Complete Guide to Pregnancy and Newborn Sleep Training

A New Mom's Survival Handbook, What to Expect in Labor, Wise Tips and Tricks for No Cry Nights and a Happy Baby

Heidi Oster

© Copyright 2019 - All rights reserved.

The content contained within this book may not be reproduced, duplicated or transmitted without direct written permission from the author or the publisher.

Under no circumstances will any blame or legal responsibility be held against the publisher, or author, for any damages, reparation, or monetary loss due to the information contained within this book. Either directly or indirectly.

Legal Notice:
This book is copyright protected. This book is only for personal use. You cannot amend, distribute, sell, use, quote or paraphrase any part, or the content within this book, without the consent of the author or publisher.

Disclaimer Notice:

Please note the information contained within this document is for educational and entertainment purposes only. All effort has been executed to present accurate, up to date, and reliable, complete information. No warranties of any kind are declared or implied. Readers acknowledge that the author is not engaging in the rendering of legal, financial, medical or professional advice. The content within this book has been derived from various sources. Please consult a licensed professional before attempting any techniques outlined in this book.

By reading this document, the reader agrees that under no circumstances is the author responsible for any losses, direct or indirect, which are incurred as a result of the use of information contained within this document, including, but not limited to, — errors, omissions, or inaccuracies.

Contents

What to Expect for First-Time Moms _____ 1

Introduction _____ 5

Chapter 1:
Pregnancy Overview _____ 7

Chapter 2:
Do's and Don'ts _____ 9

Chapter 3:
Picking an OB-GYN _____ 19

Chapter 4:
Nutrition While Pregnant _____ 29

Chapter 5:
The First Trimester Weeks 1 to 12 _____ 35

Chapter 6:
The Second Trimester Weeks 13 to 26 _____ 43

Chapter 7:
The Third Trimester Weeks 27 to 40 _____ 57

Chapter 8:
Getting Ready to Go to the Hospital _____ 67

Chapter 9:
Getting Ready for Labor: Stages of Labor _____ 77

Chapter 10:
In-Hospital Procedures Commonly Done on a Newborn _____ 91

Chapter 11:
Post Recovery _____ 95

Chapter 12:
FAQ's _____ 101

Conclusion _____ 107

Baby Sleep Guide to Promote Healthy Sleep Habits ___ 109

Introduction ___ 113

Chapter 1:
What You Need to Know About Baby Sleep ___ 115

Chapter 2:
Bedtime Problems and How to Can Fix Them ___ 127

Chapter 3:
What Is Normal Sleeping Behavior ___ 131

Chapter 4:
Tools You Need for Success ___ 139

Chapter 5:
Develop a Sleep Schedule ___ 153

Chapter 6:
Sleep with Assistance Plan (SWAP) ___ 157

Chapter 7:
Sleep Learning Independence Plan (SLIP) ___ 169

Chapter 8:
If Night Waking Starts to Happen Again? ___ 181

Chapter 9:
How to Handle Naptime Troubles ___ 189

Chapter 10:
Common Setbacks ___ 193

Conclusion ___ 203

COMPLETE GUIDE TO *Pregnancy* AND *Newborn Sleep Training*

2 MANUSCRIPTS

A NEW MOM'S SURVIVAL HANDBOOK, WHAT TO EXPECT IN LABOR, WISE TIPS AND TRICKS FOR NO CRY NIGHTS AND A HAPPY BABY

HEIDI OSTER

What to Expect for First-Time Moms

The Ultimate Beginners Guide While Expecting, Everything You Need to Know for a Healthy Pregnancy, Labor, Childbirth, and Newborn - A New Mom's Survival Handbook

Heidi Oster

Introduction

The following chapters will discuss everything that you need to know to get prepared for your pregnancy. Pregnancy is a great time, one full of excitement, and maybe a little bit of anxiety as you aren't sure what to expect. This guidebook will provide you with all the information that you need to be prepared for every step of your pregnancy.

Inside this guidebook, we are going to explore all the different parts of your pregnancy and how to be prepared. We will talk about how to pick out your OB-GYN, how to eat the right foods, what to expect during each of the different stages of the pregnancy, how to prepare for labor, and so much more!

As a first-time mother, you may be uncertain about what to expect during the pregnancy. Make sure to check out this guidebook and learn how exciting and amazing your pregnancy can be.

Heidi Oster

Chapter 1:
Pregnancy Overview

Congratulations! You're pregnant! After you have taken some time to celebrate and show off your excitement, you may be wondering what needs to be done next. As a first-time mom, you may feel overwhelmed with all the things that are on your to-do list. Some of the most important things that you need to do as you wait to meet your baby include:

Calculate the due date: You can bring out your calendar and try to figure it out, but one of the easiest ways to do it is to find a due date calculator online. It is going to tell you the date your baby is due, it can give you a calendar that shows when you can hear the heartbeat, when you find out the sex, and more.

Choose your doctor: You are going to spend a lot of time with your doctor during this time, so it is important that you find someone you see as a good match. Once you find someone, make sure you schedule your first appointment. This appointment will usually happen between six to eight weeks along.

Decide when you want to announce your pregnancy: This is different for everyone. Some will choose to tell people right away, and others may worry about the risk of a miscarriage and will wait until the first trimester is done. Some will tell family and friends but will wait to tell their boss or co-workers, because they don't want different treatment at work. You can pick the time when you tell others and even the method that you want to use.

Heidi Oster

As soon as you find out that you are pregnant, it is time to start taking care of your body. This means that you need to pay attention to your health and the foods you are eating now. You should be prepared for some of the early symptoms of pregnancy, though these are different in each person. And be aware of some of the different changes that are going to occur in your body during this time.

The important thing here is that every woman is going to be different. Just because someone else had horrible morning sickness doesn't mean that you will. And just because you are experiencing different symptoms compared to someone else doesn't mean that something is wrong. If you are ever concerned about your pregnancy, make sure to talk it over with your doctor.

Chapter 2:
Do's and Don'ts

Being pregnant can be a wonderful time. You are excitedly waiting for your new addition to come, counting down the days, wondering what they will be like and who they will grow up to be, and trying to get everything prepared. With all the new information that is coming your way, you may be confused about some of the things to expect during this new time. Let's take a look at some of the things that you should do, and some things that you should avoid, during your pregnancy.

Do Take Your Multivitamin
As we will talk about in a later chapter, eating a diet that is balanced and has plenty of healthy vitamins and minerals can be one of the best ways to provide your body with all of the healthy nutrients that you and the growing baby will need. However, your body is going through a lot right now. With that and the morning sickness that could make eating properly almost impossible, a healthy diet may not be enough.

This is why it's recommended that you take a prenatal vitamin each day. You can choose to go with a regular multivitamin, but the prenatal is often going to contain higher levels of specific nutrients that you really need when you are pregnant. Nutrients like iron, calcium, and folic acid are found in higher concentrations than regular vitamins, and they are going to help with the proper development of the fetus and can help prevent against birth defects.

Don't Smoke

Your OB-GYN should discuss this with you right away, but it is so important that you don't smoke while you are pregnant. If you are a smoker, make sure that you stop right away. Stay away from others who smoke as well.

Babies who are born to women who smoke during pregnancy are more likely to have learning disabilities and are more likely to be born at a lower weight compared to children who had mothers who didn't smoke at all. In addition, children who were born of women who smoke are more likely to experiment with smoking at a younger age and get hooked.

Try to Get Plenty of Sleep

While you are pregnant, you are likely to feel tired, like all of the time. Anxiety about the pregnancy, anticipation, and changing hormone levels can make sleep hard to come by during your nine months. Pregnancy can be really demanding, no matter which trimester you are in, and it is important for you to get the sleep that you need.

It is so important to get as much sleep as you can during the pregnancy. This means take a short nap any time that you feel tired and set a bedtime that you can stick with. Most pregnant women need to get somewhere between seven and nine hours of sleep each night. Don't feel bad if you are tired and worn down during this time. Your body is building a whole new life, and that can be exhausting. Take it easy and relax when you can.

Avid the Alcohol

Just like with the smoking that we talked about before, you also need to make sure that you avoid drinking any alcohol while you are pregnant. Alcohol can really impact the development of your baby. Women who drink any alcohol while pregnant could deliver a baby who is dealing with fetal alcohol syndrome. Symptoms of FAS could include:

- Low birth weight in the baby

- Behavior problems

- Learning disabilities

- Lagging patterns for the baby in their growth and when they hit development milestones.

The amount of alcohol does not seem to be the issue. Even smaller amounts of alcohol on occasion can still cause problems. If you run into issues with drinking during the pregnancy, it is important to talk to your doctor right away to help keep your baby healthy.

Do Add in Some Physical Activity

Sure, you may be tired and it may seem like a crazy idea to try and work out, but it is actually really good for you and for the baby. We are no longer focusing on the days when a pregnant woman needed to just sit at home and not lift a finger when they were pregnant. Exercise is good for both the mother and the baby. In addition, regular exercise during the pregnancy could help to combat many issues that come up including:

- Excessive weight gain

- Muscle pain

- Insomnia

- Mood problems

If you were someone who spent time exercising on a regular basis before you became pregnant, then it is usually fine to keep with that amount as well. You can always talk with your doctor about any of the adjustments that you may need to make to your routine. This may become more of a problem during the second and the third trimester, depending on how your pregnancy goes.

If you did not have a regular exercise routine before the pregnancy, then you should talk with your doctor about the best way to incorporate a fitness routine into your day. You will want to start out easy so that you don't cause harm to yourself or to the baby, but there is no reason that you can't start reaping the benefits of a good workout program.

Do Not Eat Any Raw Meat

Raw or any undercooked meat, as well as eggs, can carry some risk of foodborne illness. Food poisoning can also be an issue here. These conditions are hard enough on you, but they could lead to life-threatening illnesses for the baby and in some cases, if they are severe enough, could cause birth defects or a miscarriage. Make sure that all the meat and eggs that you consume while pregnant are always well cooked and prepared properly.

Eat Some Seafood

Another thing that you should consider doing when you are pregnant is to eat plenty of seafood. This seafood can be loaded with plenty of great minerals and vitamins including iron, zinc, and omega-3 fatty acids. All of these are important for baby and for mom. Make sure that when you do eat seafood though, that it is cooked all the way through.

One thing to note here is that you should make sure that you are avoiding any fish that is raw or fish that contains higher levels of mercury because these can be harmful to the baby. Some fish that do have this higher level of mercury and should be avoided includes:

- King mackerel
- Tilefish
- Swordfish
- Shark

Avoid the Deli Meats

Deli meats may be convenient and may be something that you would like to eat on a regular basis because of their ease; they are really something that you should avoid when you are pregnant. All deli meat includes cured meats, smoked salmon, sausages, and hot dogs. These can cause a variety of food-borne illnesses like toxoplasmosis and listeriosis.

If you do decide to consume these kinds of meats, make sure that you cook them through well to reduce the risk. In addition, make sure that you eat milk and cheese that are pasteurized, not raw. You can also wash all of your produce to make sure that you eliminate any harmful bacteria that are present there.

Do Not Sit Inside of a Hot Tub
Though the idea of a hot tub may seem like a great idea to relieve some of those sore muscles and any other pregnancy-related discomforts, it is not something that you should do. This means that you should avoid things like saunas, Jacuzzis, and hot tubs. Research suggests that the heat that comes from these can be harmful to the baby and there is some research that shows how using one of the above during the first trimester could double your risk of miscarriage.

Get the Flu Shot
No matter what time of year you are pregnant, it is a good idea to go out and get a flu shot. As long as you don't have any special circumstances that would make getting the flu shot a bad thing, this is perfectly healthy. Your doctor can discuss this with you. But getting the vaccine during pregnancy not only helps you, but it can also help your baby. Your baby will not be able to get the flu vaccine for their first six months of life, so getting the flu shot during the pregnancy not only helps them during the pregnancy but also afterward.

Limit the Amount of Caffeine You Consume
While you may feel that a lot of caffeine is the only way that you are going to make it through your pregnancy, you do need to be careful about how much you are taking in. Caffeine is able to travel from you through to the placenta and will increase the heart rate of the baby. There is some research out there that suggests that you can consume up to a few cups of coffee each day and be safe. But you do not want to drink nonstop coffee and the triple-shot latte while you are pregnant. Find other ways to help you stay awake during the pregnancy to ensure that you keep the baby safe.

Be Smart About Your Weight Gain

While there is a lot of talk out there that you can "eat for two" while you are pregnant, you really shouldn't take this to heart and then eat whatever you want to. Instead, you need to be a little bit strategic about what you eat and how much you eat.

While you do need to gain a little bit of weight to help support your growing baby, gaining too much weight can actually cause more harm than good to the baby. And you probably need a lot fewer calories than you think. For example, during the first trimester, you will only need to take in about 100 extra calories each day to help your baby grow, and many times, you may end up getting less depending on how hard your morning sickness is. By the third trimester, you will probably need about 300 extra calories each day.

Avoid the Litter Box

If you have a cat in the home, then you will need to be careful. It is fine for you to pet your cat all you want, as long as you wash your hands when you are done. However, you should never clean out the litter box. Feline waste actually has millions of little parasites inside. And one of them in particular, known as Toxoplasma Gondil, can be really toxic and dangerous to mothers who are pregnant and their babies.

If you contract that particular toxin, you will never know that it is there until you start to have some complications with the pregnancy. There are no signs ahead of time, and you can't do anything until it is too late. It is possible to have a stillbirth or a miscarriage from it. And babies who contract this parasite can face a lot of serious health concerns including mental disabilities and seizures to name a few of them.

Visit the Dentist

Many people are scared of going to the dentist. The American College of Obstetricians and Gynecologists recommend that a mother who is expecting go and get routine oral health, even when they are pregnant. They also recommend that you go in to get regular dental cleanings. You should make sure that your dentist knows that you are pregnant so they can make adjustments to some of the tools they are using in some cases, but otherwise, it is perfectly safe to go while you are pregnant, and in fact, it can be good for your overall health, as well as for your oral health.

Practice Some Yoga

While you do need to be careful to not start out with something insane like hot yoga or Bikram yoga, there are many types of yoga that are fine to use while you are pregnant. You should look specifically for gentle yoga or prenatal yoga so that you can get all of the benefits without having to worry about causing harm to you or the baby. If you did not spend time doing yoga before you got pregnant, you should consider looking for a class that is designed for expectant mothers. This will ensure that you are able to practice yoga in a manner that is safe and effective for your needs. Always listen to your body and see what you are able to handle without straining too much.

Do Have Sex

There are some expecting mothers who worry about having sex because they worry about what that will do to their developing baby. Sex during pregnancy is usually just fine. If you have a high-risk pregnancy or something like placenta previa, you may want to avoid sex. But for most pregnancies, it is just fine to have sex throughout. If you are worried about having sex with your partner or you have any questions about how safe intercourse is at any time during the pregnancy, then you can always talk with your doctor about your unique circumstances.

Heidi Oster

Chapter 3:
Picking an OB-GYN

One of the first things you will need to do after finding out you are pregnant is to find your OB-GYN. This is the doctor who will care for you and your baby throughout the pregnancy. But how do you know which doctor is the right one for you?

If you already see a gynecologist who can practice obstetrics as well, you can consider asking them to help take care of you during the pregnancy. You are already familiar with this doctor so there wouldn't be any changes there. Make sure that you feel comfortable with this doctor taking care of the pregnancy and that you wouldn't mind giving birth in the hospital associated with that doctor.

If your current doctor doesn't practice obstetrics, or you don't want to use your current doctor for some reason, then you can ask for a recommendation from a healthcare provider. Sometimes you can even talk to relatives or friends who recently had a baby. Childbirth educations can provide you with this information as well.

Remember that while most families in the United States choose to deliver their babies with the help of an obstetrician, there are other options you can choose. It is possible to work with a family physician, direct-entry midwives or certified nurse midwife to name a few.

What Criteria Should I Use When Choosing My Ob-Gyn?

Each woman is going to be different and you may find that some considerations are more important for you than for others. For example, if you have things that could result in a high-risk pregnancy, you may need to see a specialist and that can change the way you look for your doctor. You may need to check with your insurance provider to see who is covered in your network. Or you might rule out a doctor who goes to a hospital too far away. Some of the other factors you may want to consider when choosing an OB-GYN include:

Your Personal Health History

If you currently have any type of chronic illness, such as diabetes, heart disease, epilepsy, or high blood pressure, you may need to talk about this with your chosen doctor. You want to have someone who has had past experience caring for patients like you. And in some cases, you may need a primatologist or a maternal-fetal medicine specialist to help with the pregnancy since both of these deals with high-risk pregnancies.

The Outlook of The Doctor

It can be really uncomfortable being in a pregnancy and then finding out the doctor holds a different outlook on some important issues. Before choosing an OB-GYN, you need to find out what the attitude is for your doctor about important issues such as episiotomies, interventions like IVs, and more. During your first pregnancy, you may not be able to predict what you will need to have happened during that time, but you can talk with the doctor and get a good idea of the general approach the doctor will use when they work with you.

If you are interested in having either a doula or other support people in the delivery room with you, then you should also discuss this with your doctor. Some doctors will only allow your partner to be in the room, and you don't want to find out about this attitude when you are delivering. You can also explore if your doctor seems supportive of you having a natural childbirth (if you choose this option), and do they encourage breastfeeding?

Compatibility

Sometimes, it all comes down to how comfortable you feel with your doctor. You could have someone who is considered the best doctor around, but if you don't like how they handle some topics, or you just don't feel comfortable with them, then this is not the right doctor for you.

Pregnancy and childbirth can be very exciting, but this is also a stressful time for some first-time moms. You want to make sure that the healthcare partner you pick out is someone who makes you feel comfortable and whom you can communicate with well. Some questions that you can ask yourself about the doctor before committing include:

- How comfortable do I feel around this doctor?
- Is the doctor going to respect my wishes during this process?
- Does this doctor seem like they will be interested in me personally?
- Did I feel like the doctor took the time to explain things to me?
- Was it easy for me to ask questions to this doctor?

How Often Will I See This Doctor?

You and your OB-GYN are going to see a lot of each other over the next few months. You will see them much more than you are used to visiting any other doctor through most of your life. This is to ensure that both you and the baby are doing well during the whole pregnancy.

At some practices, you are going to see your obstetrician at all, or at least most, of your prenatal visits. You may have the option of seeing another OB or a nurse practitioner if yours is not there. It isn't a bad thing to meet the other OBs in the office if you can because it is possible one of them could deliver your baby. In some other practices, you may see a nurse practitioner for every appointment unless you end up with a complication or you have a pregnancy that is considered high-risk.

How Many Prenatal Appointments Will I Have?

If you have a healthy pregnancy with no complications, you will still have quite a few prenatal visits to check up on you and the baby. The recommended prenatal schedule for a healthy pregnancy includes:

- Between weeks 4 and 28, you will have one visit each month.

- Between weeks 28 and 36, you will have 1 prenatal visit every two weeks.

- For the last month, weeks 36 to 40, you will visit your doctor each week.

The schedule that the doctor recommends should always be followed. It is important for you and your baby to have prenatal care. There are three times more chances that a baby has low birth weight when mothers don't practice proper prenatal care. With these regular visits, the doctor is able to spot problems and treat them, giving you the healthiest pregnancy possible.

If you are considered a high-risk pregnancy, you may need to go and visit your doctor more often. This allows the doctor more time to monitor the pregnancy and make sure that it is as safe as possible. Follow the schedule that your doctor gives to you to make sure you and your baby stay as healthy as possible.

What Happens During My Prenatal Appointments?

Many of your appointments are going to go the same. Your doctor will meet with you and ask questions about how you feel emotionally and physically and whether you have any questions, worries or complaints you will like to share. Depending on how far along you are, the doctor may have some other questions they want to ask.

The prenatal visits aim is to give the information you need to keep your pregnancy healthy and check your pregnancy as well. You should go to all of these appointments, regardless of whether you are feeling fine and think that everything is going well.

During the appointment, your doctor is going to check your urine, blood pressure, and weight. They can also listen to the heartbeat of your baby, check the position of the baby, and measure your abdomen. Each pregnancy will be a bit different so there may be other exams and tests done to check how things are going. And if the doctor sees that there may be some complications, they will closely monitor that and intervene when needed.

The findings of your every checkup will be reviewed to you by the practitioner. They will give details on what will normally happen on the next few weeks and give you warning signs to watch out for. You can also spend some time talking about the benefits and negatives of some optional tests you will want to consider.

Risk Factors That May Require Me to Visit My OB-GYN

There are some risk factors that will require you to go and visit your doctor more often than normal during your pregnancy. This often depends on your individual health profile and if any complications arise during the pregnancy. Having any of the following risk factors can help the doctor decide how many visits you should make for you to take care of your pregnancy:

Being older than 35: Most women who give birth during their late 30s and early 40s will have healthy and strong babies. However, there is a higher risk of birth defects for babies who were born by mothers aged 35 and above. Several complications during the pregnancy will also be higher.

Pre-existing health problems: There are many health conditions that can cause issues during your pregnancy and can make you high-risk. The doctor will want you to have more appointments with them when you have high blood pressure and diabetes. It is their job to ensure you that your conditions won't affect the health of you and your baby. Other conditions that could require more visits include obesity, anemia, lupus, and asthma.

Medical problems that arise while you are pregnant: While you are pregnant, your doctor is going to watch out for complications that can occur. These can include preeclampsia, pregnancy-related high blood pressure, and gestational diabetes.

Risks of preterm labor: If you show signs that you will go into labor earlier than normal, the doctor is going to monitor the pregnancy more closely.

Your mind can be at ease when you have regular prenatal visits with your doctor. By doing so, you ensure that you will have a healthy pregnancy all throughout and deliver a healthy baby at the end.

Questions to Ask Before Choosing Your OB-GYN

When you are looking for an OB-GYN, there are several questions you should ask to make sure you and your doctor are on the same page. The right questions can ensure that you get the right doctor and that there aren't any surprises later on. Some of the questions that you should consider asking before you choose your OB-GYN include:

- What are your beliefs and philosophies about birth?

- Does your doctor see birth as a medical process that needs to be managed continuously?

- Do they see birth as a process that is fraught with a lot of potential issues and requires preventative procedures?

- Do they see it as a natural process where nature should be allowed to do some of the work before interfering?

- How much choice do you think you should have in the decisions for this pregnancy?

You will have a much better pregnancy experience if you can help make decisions and are given some options. Women who feel that they are not involved and have no control over what is going on are going to have a less positive experience and may experience anxiety and depression. Choose a doctor who will let you be involved.

What Are Your Thoughts About Using Pain Relief During Labor?

Does the doctor assume that you will take the pain relief like everyone else already does, or are they there to support and encourage your whichever method that you choose?

- Will the doctor inform you about any of the side effects of the medication and pain control?

- Will they encourage you to take the pain relief or give recommendations against it if you are close to birthing?

What Are Your Thoughts About the Birth Plan?

It is important to put a birth plan together early on. While things may not always go as plan, it at least lets your doctor and others know your preferences. Talk to your doctor about it and see if they see any concerns that need to be addressed.

What Is Your Induction Rate?

Each doctor is going to have a different preference when it comes to induction. Some will discuss it after your estimated due date and some will wait until a week or more after the due date. And then there are some who will induce ahead of time to meet a schedule. Find out how often the doctor induces and see if they are happy to use it too much. Inductions can cause complications in your baby and should only be used if medically necessary.

What Is Your C-Section Rate?

C-sections can lead to a longer recovery period and most of them are not necessary. Many hospitals in the United States are showing rates of c-sections of up to 70 percent. Considering only about 10 percent of c-sections are actually necessary. It is possible that you may need a c-section during your pregnancy, but you don't want to go through one, and deal with the harmful recovery time afterward, just because it is faster and more convenient for the doctor.

Some other questions you may want to ask your OB-GYN during pregnancy and at your appointments include:

- What medications over the counter are fine for me to take?

- Is it normal to have any spotting and cramping and when should I call in about it?

- How much weight am I going to gain during the pregnancy? How much weight is acceptable, and how much is too much, for me? Can I exercise when I am pregnant?

- Do I need to get vaccinated? Which vaccines do I need?

- Will I see some permanent changes in my reproductive system after I give birth?

- Will I have any issues controlling my bladder after I have the baby?

Heidi Oster

Chapter 4:
Nutrition While Pregnant

Another topic we need to explore during pregnancy is the diet you follow. You are not going to spend your time trying to lose weight and restricting your calories. While some women may lose weight during the beginning of their pregnancy because of the morning sickness, striving to lose weight while pregnant can lead to harmful health effects for the mom and the developmental delays in the baby.

Dieting to lose weight while you are pregnant can be hazardous to you and the baby. This can be really bad because it often results in a restriction of important nutrients to the baby include folic acid and iron. This is why you should avoid some of the popular diet plans, such as South Beach, The Zone, Atkins, and the Raw Food Diet while you are pregnant.

When we talk about diet while pregnant, we mean fine-tuning some of your eating habits so that you and the baby get plenty of good nutrition. Healthy eating during this time is so important to the development and growth of the baby. To get the nutrients that are needed, you must eat from a variety of food groups, while also limiting your consumption of junk foods, sugars, and processed foods. Yes, you may have a lot of different cravings during pregnancy, and it is fine to give into them on occasion, but overall, you do need to limit your consumption of these.

Remember that while you are pregnant, you do not need to eat for two. Many pregnant women fall into this mindset and then find they have put on way too much weight during their pregnancy. In the beginning, you will only need about 100 extra calories a day. During the final trimester, when the baby gets big and needs more nutrition, you can have up to an extra 300 calories each day.

The Food Groups to Eat

When you are pregnant, it is important to eat a wide variety of foods throughout the day. Doing this will make sure that you yourself and your baby the nutrients you both needs. Some of the food groups that you should concentrate on during this time include:

Fruits and Vegetables

Fresh produce contains many of the important nutrients that you need for pregnancy. They are especially high in folic acid and vitamin C. While you are pregnant, you must get in a minimum of 70 mg of vitamin C each day to help keep you healthy. You can find plenty of this nutrient in vegetables like Brussel Sprouts, tomatoes, and broccoli and in fruits like honeydew, grapefruits, and oranges.

To help prevent any neural tube defects in your baby, you need to take in 0.4 mg of folic acid every day. Dark leafy vegetables can help provide you with this folic acid, and legumes, like veal, black-eyed peas, and lima beans are good sources too. Try to get about two to four servings of fruit each day, and at least four servings of vegetables.

Bread and Other Grains

One of the main sources for energy when you are pregnant will be the carbs that are found in grains and breads. You need to make sure that you take in enriched products and whole grains because they provide the body with many great nutrients, including Iron, fiber, protein, and the B vitamins. You can sometimes get extra folic acid if you eat fortified cereals and bread.

The amount of grains that you should consume each day will depend on your weight as well as your personal dietary needs. You can have somewhere between six to eleven servings of these grains and bread each day.

Protein

Don't forget to get in plenty of protein into your diet during pregnancy. Beans, eggs, fish, poultry, and meat can all be great sources of protein. They also contain much of the iron and B vitamins that you need. Remember that not only do you need protein, but your growing baby needs it in higher amounts during the second and the third trimester. Iron is also important because it helps to carry oxygen to the baby. Your body needs oxygen as well because it moves oxygen to your muscles, which can help alleviate pregnancy symptoms like depression, irritability, weakness, and fatigue.

It is recommended that you take in about 27 mg of protein each day. There are a lot of great options when it comes to choosing where to get your protein from each day. Lean beef, liver, veal, turkey, lamb, and chicken can be good. Some types of fish and other seafood can be good, as long as you follow the right guidelines. Aim to consume a minimum of three servings of protein each day.

Dairy Products

During pregnancy, you should consume a minimum of 1000 mg of calcium each day. Calcium is so important to building up strong bones and teeth, to help with normal blood clotting, and can help with proper nerve and muscle function. Since your baby is going to need large amounts of calcium to help them grow and develop, your body will either need to get it out of your diet, or your body will take it from your own bones to support the baby.

There are many sources of calcium that you can choose to enjoy when you are pregnant. You can go with puddings, cream soups, yogurt, cheese, and milk. There is also a little bit of calcium found in options like dried peas, beans, seafood, and green vegetables. Make sure that you get a minimum of four servings of dairy each day.

Prenatal vitamins

Although most of your nutrition should come from the foods you eat, a daily prenatal vitamin can be useful. Sometimes, you may have trouble keeping your food down, such as during the first trimester, or you may have trouble eating as the baby gets bigger. A prenatal vitamin can help fill in some of the gaps if you need it.

Foods That You Should Avoid While Pregnant

While you are pregnant, there are also some foods that you need to avoid. These foods are often harmful because they have some bacteria or other issues with them that can harm the developing baby during this time. Some of the foods that you should make sure you avoid while you are pregnant include:

Deli meats: These types of meats can sometimes be contaminated with listeria, which can cause a miscarriage. These bacteria can cross the placenta and will affect the baby, causing infection or blood poisoning that can be life-threatening. If you do want to eat deli meats during this time, make sure to reheat them to avoid issues.

Fish with mercury: Mercury that is consumed, especially when it is done in high dosages, can be linked back to developmental delays and even brain damage. Some fish that you should use include tilefish, king mackerel, swordfish, and shark.

Smoked seafood: Refrigerated or smoked seafood is often labeled as jerky, kippered, nova style, or lox and you should avoid it because it is likely there is listeria in it. This is the fish that is found in the deli section so avoid that.

Raw eggs: Raw eggs can have a potential of salmonella exposure, as well as foods that are made out of raw eggs, so you should avoid them. Options like Hollandaise sauces, custards, ice creams (if they are homemade), and even mayo and Caesar dressings can be an issue because they are made with raw eggs. If the recipe has been cooked at some point, this can reduce the risk.

Soft cheese: Some soft cheeses may contain listeria. You would need to avoid these such as some Mexican style cheese, Gorgonzola, feta, and brie. All soft non-imported cheeses that have been made with pasteurized milk will be safe to eat.

Milk that is unpasteurized: These types of milk can contain listeria so make sure that you drink a form that is pasteurized.

Pate: Any type of meat spread needs to be avoided because they could contain listeria.

Caffeine. While it is fine to have this in moderation, you do need to be careful with the amount. Try to keep it down to maybe one cup of coffee, or the equivalent, each day to help you not run into pregnancy complications. Drinking too much can mean that the diuretic effects of caffeine will kick in and you could end up with calcium and water loss.

Alcohol. No amount of alcohol is safe when you are pregnant and you need to avoid it the whole time. When the mother chooses to have alcohol during the pregnancy, it could interfere with the healthy development of the baby. If the alcohol is ingested in high amounts for a lot of the pregnancy, it could result in Fetal Alcohol Syndrome and other disorders for the baby. If you did drink before you found out you were pregnant, it is important to stop now. And you should discontinue your use through the pregnancy and during breastfeeding if you choose to do it.

Chapter 5:
The First Trimester Weeks 1 to 12

There is a lot that will happen with your baby as they begin to develop. The first trimester will see a lot of changes, even if you don't see your belly growing yet. You may not look like you are pregnant at this point, but it's likely that you are feeling it by now. This is because a ton of pregnancy hormones are going to work and prepping your body to host your baby for some time now. Be prepared for a lot of pains and aches from the pregnancy, and you will probably be tired quite a bit. While you might not be all that thrilled with the symptoms that come with pregnancy, remember that most of these are going to be temporary and that you get a baby at the end.

How Long Is the First Trimester?
The first week up to the thirteen weeks of your pregnancy will be your first trimester. If you are not sure when your pregnancy is, you will need to figure out your due date. This helps you to know where you are in the pregnancy and how far you have left. Remember that it is possible for the due date to change, especially if you are someone with irregular periods.

The Growth of Your Baby During the First Trimester
There is a lot of growing that your baby will go through during this first trimester. The baby will start as a zygote, a single fertilized cell. Next, it will plant itself on the wall of the uterus as an embryo where in it will continue to

become a baby the size of a peach that already has limbs and body systems. Organs are going to start taking shape and the baby will start to move. Some of the other highlights that you will notice with your baby during this time include:

Their bones. When the baby reaches six weeks, they will start to grow feet, hands, legs, and arms. Their toes and fingers will start to grow at about ten weeks.

Hair and nails. Week 5 and 8 are when the baby will start forming its skin. Around week 11, the nail beds and hair follicles will form.

Digestive system. The intestines of the baby will begin to form by the 8th week. They will also have gone through two kidney sets, and the third, and final, set will be on the way.

Sense of touch. Your baby is going to start developing some touch receptors on their face, mostly on the nose and the lips, when they reach week 8. A few weeks later at week 12, they are going to have receptors at the soles of the feet, palms, and genitals.

Eyesight. By the time the baby is four weeks old, their optic nerves and lenses will start to form. By week 8, the retina will form as well.

Heart: By the time you get to week five, the tube that is going to be the heart will begin to beat spontaneously. It is going to become stronger and easier to hear sometime between week 9 and 10.

Brain. When your baby reaches week 8, their brain is going to get to work wiggling all those developing limbs.

Sense of taste. The baby is going to start developing taste buds and have them connected back to the brain by 8 weeks. But it will be some time before they can taste anything because they still need the taste pores.

Some of the other major changes that are going to occur in the baby during this first trimester include the development of their vocal cords, the production of white blood cells to help fight off any infections, and the formation of their muscles.

Changes in Your Own Body

A lot is going to happen to you during the first trimester as well. Some of the early pregnancy symptoms that you are going to notice during the first trimester include:

Morning sickness. For most women, this doesn't just strike in the morning. These symptoms are going to start up when you reach six weeks of pregnancy. There are different techniques that you can try to reduce the symptoms a little bit including taking ginger drops or tea. Stick with smaller meals. If the symptoms continue or seem to get worse, you can talk to your doctor about the options available.

Tender breasts. There will be some changes to your breasts when you are pregnant. You may notice that they get bigger, are tingly, and tender. This usually happens around week 6.

Mood swings. You may find that your mood is going to change often when you are pregnant. One moment you may be up, another time you may be down, and the next it can go all over the place. This is perfectly normal.

As the pregnancy progresses through this trimester, you may notice that there are lots of other pregnancy symptoms that come up. Each woman is different, but some of the symptoms that you may notice include headaches, food aversions, and a metallic taste in the mouth, constipation, and heartburn. The good news is that when you enter the second trimester, you should be able to get some relief from these symptoms.

Weight Gain

During this stage, your baby is still really small. This means that you are not going to gain much weight during this time. You should stick with three to four pounds of weight gain during the first trimester. If you have really bad morning sickness and can't keep food down, you may end up losing a little weight. This is fine, as long as you are able to pick up those pounds later on. For now, you should focus on eating meals that are light, but eat them more often, and make sure the foods you pick are high in nutrients. Crackers, whole grain bread, bananas, yogurt, and avocados can be great options to give you nutrients but can be gentle on the stomach as well.

For some women, they are extra hungry when they are in the first trimester. Try to keep your calorie intake in check during all parts of your pregnancy. The first trimester won't necessarily require you to have extra calories. If you do end up getting more pounds put on than is recommended during the first trimester, do not fret though. Just focus your energy on getting back on track during the rest of the pregnancy.

Symptoms You Should Have Checked Out by Your Doctor

It will be hard to know what is normal and what isn't during your pregnancy because of your body will have many different changes. In many cases, the odd twinge or a bit of pain here or there is not a big deal. However, the first trimester is going to have a higher risk of miscarriage than the others. Some of the symptoms that you should be aware of and call your doctor about will include:

- Disturbances in your vision

- Severe puffiness that shows up in the face and hands

- A fever that gest over 101.5 degrees along with chills and a backache.

- Painful urination

- A sudden thirst

- Severe abdominal pain

- Heavy vaginal bleeding.

If you do experience some of the symptoms that are listed above, it is imperative that your doctor should be notified immediately. If you are not able to talk to them right away, then you need to head to your closest ER to get help for you and the baby.

Things to Do During the First Trimester
Start your prenatal vitamin: If you haven't already started taking one ahead of the pregnancy, then now is the time to do it. The development of neural tube defect will be reduced when you take prenatal vitamins during the first trimester.

Choose your doctor: There are many different types of doctors you can choose for your pregnancy. You can work with a family physician, midwife, and OB-GYN. Take your time to look at all the options that are out there and then pick the one that best fits your needs.

Book your first appointment: You need to get this appointment done sometime between six to eight weeks. Your doctor will need to take a look at your medical history and will perform a thorough exam. You will probably go through a lot of test including a urinalysis, blood work, a Pap smear, and more. You may even get an initial ultrasound to help date the pregnancy, to check the progress of your baby, and to hear the heartbeat. While the doctor is going to ask you a lot of questions here, you should take the time to ask your own questions as well.

Consider getting some genetic testing done: There are many different types of genetic screenings that you can get done to help you be aware of what may be there with your baby. Some are noninvasive and others are more invasive. You can make a decision on whether you want to do these and which ones based on personal preferences and your family history. Taking these tests can help you be prepared for what you can expect with your baby.

Look into your health insurance: The price that you pay for your pregnancy is going to vary based on many factors such as who you visit, how many appointments you have, where you give birth, and more. You should have insurance by now or sign up for one. Look at the co-insurance and the premiums to see if you can keep your costs as low as you can.

Make a budget: When you grow your family, it is a good time to take a look at your monthly expenses and see what you can do to make sure you stay within your budget.

Eat right: Cut down on your caffeine and learn which foods you should limit as much as possible. This is an important time of growth for your baby so you need to eat foods that are high in nutrients and will keep you healthy.

Keep active: You don't have to run a marathon or anything at this point, but getting up and moving, even if it is just a nice walk outside, can do wonders when it comes to keeping you healthy, helping the baby grow, and ensuring that you feel better. It is recommended that very week; you should have physical activity for at least 30 minutes.

If you feel up to it, go ahead and have sex: Sex is allowed and just fine while pregnant, and it is safe for baby. And it can have some benefits for you as well.

Consider some baby names: While you still have plenty of time before you find out what gender you are having, this can still be a good time to start considering baby names that you will want to use.

Plan out how to announce your news: Think about when and how you would like to tell others about the news. Most women will wait until they get to the end of their first trimester to do this, but you can do it at any time that you want. You should also consider when you want to tell your boss about the pregnancy. Look up the pregnancy rules in your business to help you know what to expect.

The first trimester is an important stage of your pregnancy. The baby is developing quickly, and your body is changing as well. Make sure to schedule your first prenatal appointment early on and talk with your doctor about any concerns that you have about this pregnancy.

Heidi Oster

Chapter 6:
The Second Trimester Weeks 13 to 26

When you enter the second trimester, you are going to definitely start to see some changes in your body. The next three months are going to show a lot of changes in your baby and hopefully, the welcome relief from some of those morning sickness symptoms. For most women, the second trimester is the most comfortable one of the three. You will notice that most of your early pregnancy symptoms are going to ease up a bit, and they will disappear. You will probably not feel as queasy anymore and food may start to taste better. Your energy levels will be better and by the end, you may start to see the little bulge in your tummy that looks like the beginnings of your pregnant belly.

How the Baby Grows During the Second Trimester?
The second trimester goes from week 13 to week 26 of your pregnancy. Your baby is going to be very busy during this trimester. By the time you get to the 18th week, the baby may way as much as a chicken breast and they can do a variety of actions including hiccup and yawn. But the time you get to week 21, little jabs and kicks will be felt because of their limbs moving around. And by week 23, the baby will start to pack on the weight. In fact, for the next four weeks, the baby is going to double their weight. By the time you get to the end of the second trimester, your baby will be about two pounds. Let's look at some of the other changes that may occur to your baby during the second trimester.

Hair, nails, and skins: When you reach week 16, the initial tiny hairs of the baby will start to show up. By the 22nd week, they should have eyebrows and eyelashes. The skin is now going to be covered in a downy fur coat, lanugo that is meant to keep them warm until they add more fat later on. And at week 21, the vernix caseosa, a greasy layer of oil that is meant to shield the skin, will show up. Both of these are going to shed off before the baby is born.

The digestive system: The digestive system of the baby will be formed fully by the time you end the first trimester. Now, the baby starts to swallow and suck in preparation to the world outside their mother's womb. They can even start to taste the foods that you are eating via your amniotic fluid. Because of this, the baby will even develop preferences based on your food choices when they are born. Choosing to eat healthy foods can help influence your baby to enjoy these same foods when they are older. In addition, the baby's waste systems are hard at work as well. The baby pees inside of the womb as well because of all that swallowing they do to get the required nutrition by the placenta.

Senses: The baby eyes and ears are working to move into the correct position, by the time the baby gets to week 22 of the pregnancy. These developing senses mean that the baby starts to hear, smell, and see, and they will start opening their eyes.

Heart: When the baby reaches 17 weeks, their heart will start beating on its own rather than spontaneously. The brain is able to control and regulate the heartbeat. Using a stethoscope by week 20, you can hear their heartbeat as well. During the 25th week, the capillaries are going to begin forming so that they are able to carry the blood around the body.

Brain: In addition to being able to control the heartbeat of your baby, and of inducing kicks, the brain is able to start getting the eyelids to blink by 26 weeks.

Changes in Your Body During This Trimester

While there are many changes that happen with your baby during this second trimester, there will also be some changes that occur in your body as well. The third trimester can bring up some symptoms from the first one, such as constipation and heartburn. As your belly keeps on growing and your hormones from pregnancy keep rising, there are some other symptoms that can show up including:

Congestion. As the blood flow starts to increase to the mucous membranes of the body, you may find that you're snoring for the first time. Some over the counter medications can be fine to use to resolve this issue.

A little swelling of the feet and ankles. This can happen in about seventy-five percent of women who are pregnant and it usually starts around the 2^{2nd} week. Some women may experience this issue a little bit earlier. To help reduce the puffiness, you should try to keep active when you can and then kick up the feet during any time you sit down. Try to avoid long periods of sitting or standing and always sleep on your side.

Sensitive gums. This can include a little bit of bleeding as well. Make sure to talk to your dentist during this time. If the gums easily bleed and are bright red in color, this might be a sign that you are dealing with gingivitis, and you need to visit your doctor.

Leg cramps. These can start during the second trimester and could last all the way to the third. This is due to both your hormones and the extra weight. And since some pregnant women may be short on magnesium and calcium, this problem could be worse. Make sure that you eat a diet that is well-balanced and healthy during your pregnancy.

Dizziness. Sometimes, pregnant women can experience low blood pressure. This is going to happen because of all that extra blood the body is trying to pump through. Make sure to drink plenty of fluids, eat plenty of small meals, and then take it easy.

Achiness in your lower stomach. This is sometimes referred to as round ligament pain. The ligaments that are supporting the belly are trying to stretch out to support the growing size of your belly.

Varicose veins or hemorrhoids. These can often shrink or even go away after pregnancy, especially if they weren't something that you dealt with before.

All of the above are considered normal during your pregnancy and they are often temporary. You may also have feelings of irritability, apprehension, frustration, and forgetfulness during this time as well.

The second trimester can bring big changes to your bedroom as well. Your sex life can be affected due to different changes that you and your partner should cope such as fatigue and nausea that can really kill the mood. However, there are some women who are going to find that they want sex more during this time. Communication is the key here to make sure that you avoid any resentment from either partner.

Weight Gain

You will start to put on more weight during the second trimester. You will start to gain weight in these next few months of your pregnancy. Your appetite is likely to increase, or it can reappear if it went away during your first trimester, to help support the growing baby. If you started out this pregnancy at a normal weight, you should gain about one pound each week, for a total of 14, during this trimester.

Symptoms You Should Check with Your Doctor On

The next few months of the second semester will relatively be a smooth ride for most women. However, there are some symptoms that can show up and if you do experience them, you should call your doctor. These include severe abdominal pain, vaginal bleeding, and a fever that is over 101.5 degrees.

This is also the time when you and your doctor will watch out for signs of gestational diabetes. This disease can start sometime between 24 and 28 weeks of the pregnancy. You may notice extreme fatigue, snoring, frequent copious urination, and extreme thirst. If you notice severe swelling, vision changes, or a sudden increase in weight, this could be a sign that you are dealing with preeclampsia.

Things to Do When You Enter the Second Trimester

The best thing that you can do during your second trimester is to make sure that you get plenty of rest, exercise regularly, and eat well. Some of the other things that you need to do during the second trimester include:

Prepare yourself for some routine monitoring: At each checkup that you do during this time, your doctor is going to do some monitoring of the baby. This includes checking the size of the uterus, checking your weight, checking out the height of your fundus, or the top of your uterus, and the baby's heartbeat. The doctor checks out all of this to ensure that the baby is growing properly and everything is going well.

Schedule your level two ultrasound: Usually, somewhere between weeks 18 and 22 of the pregnancy, the doctor is going to use an ultrasound to check on the baby. This gives them a more accurate idea of how big the baby is, how their major organs are developing properly, to determine the level of amniotic fluid, and you can even find out the gender of your baby.

Do your glucose screening: About one out of every ten pregnant women will be diagnosed with gestational diabetes. This is why the American College of Obstetricians and Gynecologists will recommend that you should be screened between 24 and 28 weeks pregnant. If the test comes back as positive for the extra glucose, it doesn't always mean that you have this disease. You will need to go through another set of testing to make sure. If you do have gestational diabetes, your doctor is going to refer you to a nutritionist who can help you create a meal plan and teach you to have to keep track of your levels of blood sugar.

Consider prenatal screening: This is a matter of personal preference. There are many women who go through their pregnancies without these tests. But if you have some risk factors or a family history, or if you just want to be prepared in case there is something, then you may want to go through a genetic testing.

Get your immunization: If you are pregnant during the winter or during the flu and cold season, make sure that you get your flu shot. Many times, it is recommended that you get the Tdap vaccine sometime during your third trimester because this helps to protect your baby against a whooping cough when they are born.

Shop for maternity clothes: Once the baby bump starts to show, you will need to get some new clothes to fit with them. Make sure to go for comfort, and get things a little bit bigger because that baby bump is just going to get bigger when you go into the third trimester.

Make sure that you sleep on your side: Sleeping on your side is the best when you are pregnant. You don't want to sleep on your stomach because this can add a lot of pressure to your baby and sleeping on your back can cause pressure on your back and your other organs.

Decide whether you want to find out the gender of the baby. During your anatomy scan, you get the option of finding out whether you are having a baby girl or boy. You can also choose to not find out at all. Consider whether you want to find out or if you want to be surprised when the baby is born.

Make your workouts a priority: Given all of the benefits that can come from a good workout program when you are pregnant, it is good to keep up with it during this time. Find a method that is good during pregnancy. Just make sure that you avoid any type of activities that aren't seen as safe for the belly, such as riding a bike or kickboxing.

Take in a few more calories: You do not need to start eating for two here, but you do need to increase how many calories you eat by a little bit to help support the baby. You will need to take in about 300 extra calories during the second trimester, which is like an extra snack or a few extra servings of product.

Track your weight gain: This is something that your doctor will help you out with by measuring when you go to your prenatal visits. At this point, you need to be steadily gaining weight. The doctor will have you keep track each week to make sure that you are staying in your limits without gaining too much.

Do some fun preparing things for your baby: Think about getting a bump shot? This is a photo shoot that shows off your baby bump before they are born. This is a good time to schedule the shot so you can get the time that you want. You can also consider taking a babymoon for your first child. Since your first-trimester nausea will be quelled, and because many airlines have restrictions on flying later in your pregnancy, the second trimester is the best option to take this trip. And you can consider what you want to add to your baby registry.

Look into some childbirth classes: While you probably won't start one of these classes until you reach the third trimester, it is a good idea to look into these classes now. This helps you to find a class that will work well for you.

Think about where you would like to give birth to your baby. Are you interested in giving birth at home, in a birthing center, or in a hospital? The answer to this question will determine a lot of things about the birth of your baby. Take some time to look into your options now. The birth centers and hospitals will often invite you to take a tour in your third trimester to help you be familiar with your surroundings, but you can do this earlier on as well.

Look into your childcare options: If you do plan to go back to your work after maternity leave is done, then it is never too early to look into some of the childcare options near you. There are many options such as a relative, babysitter, nanny, and daycare. The option you choose may depend on your personal preferences, how many hours you work, and your budget concerns.

Think about your baby shower: Traditionally, the mom to be doesn't host their own baby shower. Usually, a friend or family member will host this baby shower. But there is nothing wrong with letting your host know if you have any preferences in the theme or what is done at the baby shower. Make sure that your baby registry is done ahead of time so that well-wishers can pick out a gift.

Consider names: If you found out the gender of your baby, you will be able to narrow down the list of names that you like to correspond with the gender of your baby. There isn't a rush. You still have time to pick out a name. Some parents like exploring and narrowing down the names once they know the gender of their baby.

The second trimester is an exciting time. This is the trimester when most mothers are excited about the arrival of their baby. They have gotten through their morning sickness and some of the early morning pregnancy troubles are gone. They are able to enjoy their pregnancy and showing off their new baby bump to others. Enjoy this time. It is fun to watch your little one grow and develop like never before.

Genetic Testing

During your second trimester, you may choose to do some genetic testing. This kind of testing can be a good way to look closer at the health of your baby. Some tests are there to check the baby for a variety of medical conditions while you are still carrying them. Others are going to check the DNA to see if they carry some genetic diseases. Even before the pregnancy, it is possible for the mother and father to get a genetic carrier screening to look and see what the chances are that one of their children would get a genetic disorder.

Most of these tests are completely optional and parents can choose whether they want to get them done or not. Some parents do these in order to help them make better health decisions and to have a better idea of what they can expect when the baby arrives. Let's take a look at some of the different tests you may want to consider during the second trimester.

Triple Screen or Quad Screen

This screening is usually done sometime between fifteen and twenty weeks. These two types of multiple marker tests will check the levels of certain proteins and hormones in the bloodstream of the mother. Like other forms of screening that you may have done in the first trimester, these are noninvasive and can be done by getting the mother's blood sample.

The levels of proteins and hormones are measured from this sample of blood to help the family know how likely it is that the baby will have neural tube defects, trisomy 18, Down Syndrome, or issues with the development of the abdominal wall.

You will not have to go through a lot of preparation for this one. You just need to show up at the scheduled time to get the blood drawn. The lab and your doctor will take care of the rest.

Amniocentesis

This test is usually done sometime between fifteen and eighteen weeks, although it can be done any time that the doctor would like. It is more of a diagnostic test, which means that it can provide you with accurate information about the genetics of your baby. But it is much more invasive compared to the other options.

In addition to being able to diagnose some genetic abnormalities in your baby, this test can help you figure out other problems such as cystic fibrosis, sickle cell disease, spina bifida, and more. This test is able to detect neural tube defects about 99 percent and all genetic abnormalities 100 percent, so it is an accurate test, but invasive.

This test is done with an ultrasound. The doctor uses this to help locate the placenta and where the baby is. Then some local anesthetic is used to the area where they will insert the needle through the stomach and into your uterus. They can now remove a small amniotic fluid sample around the fetus. After this is done, you may feel a few menstrual like cramps.

Anatomy Ultrasound

This one happens sometime between eighteen to twenty-two weeks of pregnancy. This is often a standard of prenatal care that most women in the United States will use. It can help the doctor get a full look at the anatomy of the baby and is often done around twenty weeks. By this point, the major organs of the baby should be developed well and the doctor is able to see everything well.

Ultrasounds that are done earlier than the 22-week mark may need another ultrasound depending on how well the doctor is able to see everything. Usually, if the ultrasound is done at the 20th week, the doctor is able to visualize things just fine and you will only need one. This is the time where the doctor will notice if there seem to be any abnormalities and will also be able to tell the parents if they are having a boy or a girl.

CBC Blood Test

This test is done somewhere between 24 and 26 weeks. This blood test is standard and will take a look at your iron levels, thyroid function, and your vitamin D status. These are important to keep in a good range as you go through your pregnancy because they will help keep the baby strong. This procedure is done with a simple blood draw.

Glucose Screening

Your doctor will discuss this one with you as you get closer. It is usually done sometime between 24 and 28 weeks. The glucose screening, or the diabetes test as it is often called, is done in order to determine if a mother is suffering from gestational diabetes. You need to check for this during your pregnancy because leaving it uncontrolled can result in problems for you or the baby.

Women who are dealing with gestational diabetes are often likely to have large babies and can suffer a lot of problems during the delivery, including trouble with breastfeeding and dystocia, where the shoulder of the baby gets stuck. The babies can have a problem after they were born with blood sugar and may can possibly have diabetes in the future if they were born to mothers that have gestational diabetes.

A Glycol drink is used in this type of test. This drink is going to contain about 50 grams of sugar to do the test, although there are some midwives who are moving to orange juice or even jelly beans to do this test because they are a little tastier and easier on the system. With the Glycol drink, many mothers can feel sick and have a hard time with it, even if they don't suffer from gestational diabetes.

Either way, you will take the drink or the other sugary product on an empty stomach. After an hour has passed, your blood is drawn to help you determine your glucose level. Women who actually have gestational diabetes are going to have higher levels of glucose in their blood after the hour is done. If the test came out in the intermediate range, they will have to do this test again after three hours to check if they really have this issue.

To prepare, you need to go on a small fast before the screening. This ensures that none of the other foods you eat during the day will mess with the results. This is why most doctors will schedule this test right away in the morning. Have some options on hand for after the test, such as some bread or crackers, so that you can fill up your stomach when the blood test is done. Some women have had trouble with nausea and feeling sick while they take the drink, so discuss this with your doctor if you think it is going to be a concern.

If you have been able to stay on a healthy diet plan and maintain your exercise program throughout the pregnancy, then this should not be a problem for you. You can go through and do the test once and then be able to enjoy the rest of your pregnancy.

Heidi Oster

Chapter 7:
The Third Trimester Weeks 27 to 40

Welcome to the third trimester. At this point, you and your baby are about two-thirds of the way to the end. But there is still a lot of growing that your baby needs to do. It may feel at some points that there isn't a way that your belly will grow anymore. But as the baby keeps growing, your belly will grow to accommodate them as well. Here are some of the things that you can expect from the third trimester of the pregnancy.

The third trimester is going to begin during week 27 and will last until the baby is born. This can vary based on each person. Some mothers will give birth a little bit early, some will give birth right at forty weeks, and some will give birth after their due date. But the third trimester will continue going until the baby is born. In some cases, when the baby goes past the due date, you may be induced. This usually happens when you are really overdue and has reached the week 42 of your pregnancy. In the meantime, you have to get through the rest of the third trimester. The good news is that you are almost to the finish line here.

How the Baby Grows During This Time

Your baby will get bigger during the third trimester. They will grow from about two and a half pounds and sixteen inches long during the 28th week to somewhere between six to nine pound and between 19 to 22 inches long when you give birth at 40 weeks. Your baby is going to grow fast so don't be surprised when they run out of the room, and this leads to some really strong pokes and kicks in your gut.

There are a lot of things to be excited about when you reach the third trimester. Some of the highlights that you can look forward to with your baby during this time include:

The bones. As your baby starts to turn their cartilage over to bone in months seven and eight, they will start to get a lot of calcium from you. This is why it is so important during the third trimester to get plenty of foods with lots of calcium.

Hair, nails, and skin. By the time you reach the 32nd week of pregnancy, the baby's skin, which was see-through before, is going to become opaque. Then when you reach week 36, the fat will continue to accumulate on the baby, and they will have the nice plump skin that you are going to cuddle when they are born.

Digestive system. The baby's first poop, the meconium, will start to build up in the intestines in the final few weeks of the pregnancy. This waste is going to be a mix of lanugo, vernix, and blood cells.

The five senses. First, the touch receptors of the baby are going to develop when you reach week 29. By the 31st week of pregnancy, the baby is going to be able to get signals from all the senses. It can perceive the differences between dark and light, can taste what you eat, and can listen to the sounds that are around them.

Brain. During this time, the brain of the baby is going to start growing faster than ever before. They will start trying out some new skills such as regulating their own body temperature, dreaming, and even blinking.

When you get close to your 34ths week of the pregnancy, the body of the baby will turn southward so that they are settled with their head down and the bottom up. There are times when the baby won't turn around and will remain in a breech position. Around week 37, the doctor can manually turn the baby if they remain in the breech position.

Changes That Occur in Your Body

You will notice a great deal of fetal activity while the baby continues to grow and keeps busy inside you. Your body will have some changes as the baby get bigger than ever. Some of the different changes that you will notice during this time include:

Abdominal achiness. As your round ligaments, or the ones that are responsible for supporting your lower abdomen, start to stretch out to help hold onto that growing bump, it is likely that you are going to feel a sharp pain or cramps. The best thing that you can do for this is to take it easy.

Fatigue. Your body will find it hard to manage the demands of your pregnancy making you feel more tired. Try to get as much sleep as possible, stay active, and eat well to help avoid this issue.

Heartburn. In the final few weeks of pregnancy, the uterus is going to work and grow, which is going to push your stomach, as well as the contents inside, upward. This can cause a lot of heartburn for mom. If this problem is really bothering you, you may need to talk to your doctor about taking some medication to get relieved.

Braxton Hicks contractions. As the body works to prepare you for labor, you may feel a few irregular contractions. They may be a little bit uncomfortable, but they are not dangerous. They are simply a way for the body to prepare for the real thing.

Varicose veins. Some pregnant women notice that they have bulging veins in their lower body because of all the extra blood they are pumping around. The good news is that women who didn't have these before the pregnancy are unlikely to have them after the pregnancy is done.

Stretch marks. These are tiny little tears in the body because the skin is being stretched during the pregnancy. These are usually genetic, which is why some people get them really bad and others don't. Pick out a good moisturizer to help minimize the effects.

Backache. As the relaxion, a type of hormone, loosens up your joints and your growing belly pulls the center of gravity of the whole body forward, you will notice that you have an achy back. This is another reason that you should consider putting your feet up as much as possible.

Crazy dreams. Some women who are pregnant will also have crazy dreams. This is another result of crazy pregnancy hormone. Your dreams may be more vivid as you draw near the due date. This is normal.

Clumsiness. Your hormones are going to be on overdrive, you are going to be forgetful more than ever, and your belly is throwing it off balance. You are in good company. Clumsiness is something that many people deal with during the pregnancy. Just be careful and have some humor with it.

Lack of bladder control. You may want to start working on your Kegel exercises now. These will help keep you strong and can prevent a leaky bladder in the process.

Leaky breasts. Your body already knows that it will now have to feed the baby that is why it is starting to warm up. This can sometimes lead to leaky breasts if the milk comes in a bit early.

The third trimester can be hard on a first-time mom. The baby is getting big and between that extra weight from holding the baby and all the pregnancy hormones, the third trimester may feel like it is going on forever. But the finish line is almost here, and with a few more appointments and a few more weeks, you will be holding your new bundle of joy.

Symptoms That You Should Call Your Doctor About

As your due date nears, you may find that there are some symptoms of false labor that you will experience. These false signs of labor are simply your body preparing for the baby to come and they are nothing to be concerned about. However, there are a few symptoms that you need to be aware of because they are actually signs of true labor. The different signs that you should watch out for when you enter the later parts of the third trimester include:

Lightening. When you reach week 36, you may find that the baby drops down into the pelvis and you will start waddling a bit as you walk.

Blood show. This stringy mucus is going to be tined either brown or pink with some blood and it is a sign that your labor is on its way. You may or may not notice that there is a mucous plug that comes out as well. This plug is the part that seals the uterus from the outside world and when it comes out, it means that labor is coming.

Labor contractions. Compared to the Braxton Hicks contractions that some people experience, these will not diminish but rather intensify more, especially when you move.

Your water breaks. This may not happen until you are at the hospital and about to push. Each woman is different. But if you do notice that your water breaks when you are at home, you should head into the doctors right away.

Your doctor will also discuss with you the best times to call them or head into the hospital to be safe. When your active labor has started and your contractions have become more regular, you will definitely need to head into the hospital because the baby is coming.

If, at any time during your third trimester, you start to experience heavy vaginal bleeding or a fever that is higher than 101.5 degrees, or you experience sudden weight gain, pain in the lower stomach, or signs of preterm labor, then you should call your doctor. It is fine to trust your instincts when you experience any symptoms that seem wrong to you.

Things to Do During the Third Trimester

The third trimester is an exciting time. There is so much going on that you need to keep track of. Not only is your baby growing like crazy, but you are also dealing with the different aches and pains that come with this part of pregnancy, and you are preparing your home and your life for the new baby. Some of the things that you can do when you enter the third trimester include:

Keep track of fetal movements: Once you reach 28 weeks, you will want to count the baby's kicks on a regular basis and then note any changes to the activity during that time. This is especially true when you are in the 9th month.

Watch your weight: After you get into the third trimester, your weight gain is going to pick up speed a bit. But it is going to taper down as you get closer to your due date. Some women even report that they lose weight in the end because they eat a healthy diet and the exertion of being pregnant can be hard.

Keep moving: This can be hard now that you have the added weight from the baby, but it is important to keep active as much as possible. For most women, it is just fine to be up and moving as much as possible to help with pregnancy symptoms and to keep you fit. If there is some reason that you should be on bedrest or if there is another issue during this time, your doctor will discuss it with you.

Schedule the checkups for the third trimester: You are going to go through tests like group B strep, anemia, and glucose levels at this time. There will also be an internal examination of your cervix during the final few months to see if you are dilating or effacing at all. The doctor can schedule a nonstress stress if you are a high-risk pregnancy in the final few weeks to make sure that everything is going well.

Take a tour of the hospital: If you didn't do this during your second trimester, then this is the perfect time to do it. Seven months is a great time to look through the birthing center or hospital.

Choose your baby's pediatrician: You should have a few candidates that you want to interview with. Try to meet with them around week 32 and ask them a bunch of questions to see if they are the right one for you.

Buy the baby gear that you need: Make sure that you have all the baby gear that is needed ahead of time. Things like a car seat (the hospital won't let you leave there without having one), stroller, crib, diapers, monitor, and more.

Get educated: A birth class is essential to take in these final weeks. This is very helpful to prepare you more for your entire birth process. You can take birthing classes, take CPR classes, and baby care.

Prepare to breastfeed if you want to do this: There are a lot of benefits to breastfeeding, which is why it is such a great choice for many people. If you choose to breastfeed, you should make sure you are prepared. Take a look at the resources out there to be prepared for breastfeeding and consider getting some of the supplies such as a pump and more.

Learn about the different stages of labor: As you get closer to your due date, the idea of labor may be a scary one for many mothers. But labor is perfectly normal and it is important to know what to expect. Having this information can make it easier to prepare for when the labor actually starts.

Check the birth plan: Talk to your doctor about some of the things that you want to have happened during the birthing process. It is always nice to have a plan in place ahead of time so you make sure that people follow your wishes. But remember that sometimes things change, and you need to be flexible.

Stock up the fridge: One of the best things that you can do for yourself is to make some freezer meals before the baby is born. You are going to spend a lot of time taking care of a baby and recovering after they are born. You don't want to also cook the meals. While some friends and family may drop of meals on occasion, it can be relaxing to know that you have a large supply of healthy meals sitting there and ready to go and that you don't have to cook.

Plan out finances: Your finances are going to change quite a bit when you have a baby. Consider the costs of having a baby and how it is going to affect you financially and come up with a new budget.

Pack your hospital bag. We will discuss this one a bit more soon, but you want to bring along a few necessities, such as clothes to change into, your toothbrush, and more.

Arrange for cord blood banking: If this is something that you have been considering, then this is the time to do it. Make sure that your doctor is aware of these plans so that you get everything that you need. Make sure that you pack any cord blood kit the bank sends with you when you go to the hospital.

The third trimester is an exciting phase for many new mothers. They are excited to meet their new baby, and when they combine this with the aches and pains that come with pregnancy in the third trimester, many are ready for it to be done. Make sure that you get to all of your prenatal appointments and that you follow any recommendations that your doctor gives to you to make sure you finish the pregnancy strong.

Heidi Oster

Chapter 8:
Getting Ready to Go to the Hospital

As you get to the end of your pregnancy, you are probably getting even more excited about becoming a parent. You want to make sure that everything is as perfect as possible, but you may not know where to start. Here are some ways that you can prepare yourself when you are getting to the end of your pregnancy.

Packing Your Hospital Bag

As you get into the last few weeks of your pregnancy, you will be anxiously awaiting when your baby arrives. One of the things that you might want to consider doing is packing up your hospital bag. You are going to spend a few days in the hospital; about one to three for mothers of vaginal deliveries and three to five days for c-sections, as long as everything goes well. You don't want to end up at the hospital without something that is important or something that you need during that time. Working on your hospital bag can make it easier to be comfortable while you stay in the hospital with your baby.

Each woman is going to be a bit different in what they want to bring to the hospital with them. You can always pick out what you think is the best for your needs. Make sure that you bring along some of your necessities, such as your toothbrush and toothpaste, deodorant, and shower supplies. Some of the other things that you may want to consider putting into the bag include:

- *A dressing gown*: If you plan to walk up and down the halls during early labor, this can be helpful. Since many hospitals are warm, you may want to pick out one that is lightweight. Go with a darker color or one that is busy to help hide stains during this time.

- *Slippers*: Pick ones that are backless so that you can get them on and off easier.

- *Socks*: Sometimes, women complain of feet that are cold during labor.

- *Lotion or massage oil*: This can be useful if you want to be massaged during the labor.

- *Lip balm*: In a warm labor ward, it is likely that your lips will dry out fast. Bring some lip balm to avoid discomfort.

- *Snack and drinks*: These can be nice for something to eat after labor. Some hospitals will allow you to have snacks during labor but check ahead of time.

- *Things to pass the time or help you relax*: These can be nice during labor because they help you to focus on something other than the actual labor. They can also be nice while you are in the hospital healing. Some things that you can bring along include music, a computer, magazines, and books.

- *A going home outfit*: You will want to have some comfortable clothes that are a little loose to wear in the hospital and on the way home. You can also bring a home outfit for the baby to come home in.

- *Baby car seat.* Hospitals in the United States won't let you head home without a car seat so make sure you have it there with you.

- *Nursing bras.* It is best to bring at least a few of these with you.

- *Diapers.* The hospital may provide a few of these, but bring some just in case.

Your chosen baby blankets. Many babies like to cuddle with a blanket and their moms, and if it is cold outside when you leave the hospital, you will be glad you have this.

- Breast pads

- Maternity pads

- A few sleepsuits or other outfits that you want the baby to wear.

- Hat, socks, and booties.

These are just a few of the things that you may want to consider adding to your hospital bag. Get this prepared a few weeks ahead of time in case labor starts before your 40 weeks are done. Then you can just grab the bag and head out the door, knowing that everything you will need is right there with you.

Writing Your Birthing Plan

One thing that a lot of expectant mothers like to focus on is writing out a birth plan. This is definitely something that you should discuss with your doctor, perhaps during the second trimester, to see how many of your requests are reasonable and that the doctor will try to accommodate. This gives many women a sense of power over the situation and can make it easier on the mother heading into the experience.

The first step is to get out a journal and write down as many plans and thoughts that come to your head about the upcoming birth. This journal is going to be used to help you establish what is a priority and can give you a list of thoughts that will make the birth plan easier to create.

Your birth plan is a simple statement, one that is usually about one page, that talks about the preferences that you would like to see during the birth of your child. You can then provide a copy of this to everyone who will be in contact with you during the delivery.

Now, this is not a way to go through and write out a big list of demands to the doctor and the medical staff. It is simply a way to make sure that the doctors are aware of what you would like. Many mothers may say they want to do an all-natural birth, with no medications. Some may request that they get to have time with skin to skin contact with their baby before any tests are done. It is not acceptable to have a birthing plan that is twenty pages long though.

Also, it is important to remain as flexible as possible about the desires you have, because there are many times when things don't go according to your plan. Yes, you may wish to have a natural birth without any interventions, but when the baby goes into distress, your doctor may need to do an emergency c-section. The birthing plan can be a great way to ensure others know your preferences, but remember that childbirth is not always predictable and your birthing plan may not get followed exactly.

Picking Out Birthing Classes

There are many types of birthing classes that you can consider. Each one is going to be a bit different, and the one you go with may have to do with your birthing plan or how you want to do your birth experience. Many hospitals offer up a general birthing class that can give you a lot of the basics. But there are also several methods that you can consider, and which can be helpful during labor as well. Let's take a look at some of these options and see which one you like the best.

The Lamaze Technique
This is the first type of child birthing class you may want to consider. Lamaze is one of the most widely used methods that are used in the United States because the approach that it gives mothers to childbirth is healthy and natural. Lamaze doesn't discourage or support the use of medical interventions or other medicines that can be used during your labor and delivery, which is part of why it is so popular to use. Instead, it is there to inform mothers about all of their options so they can make the right decision for themselves, rather than being pushed one way or the other.

One of the main focuses of Lamaze is to help build up your confidence about childbirth and helping you to keep the birth of your baby as safe and simple as possible. There are often breathing techniques that are taught as well which can help you through the pain of contractions, whether you are using medicine or not with your experience.

The classes for Lamaze are usually pretty small and will be a minimum of 12 hours. These classes often touch on topics such as:

- Healthy lifestyle choices both during and after birth

- Breastfeeding

- Medical procedures

- Effective skills to use with a communication

- Getting the right support during labor

- How to practice staying relaxed during labor by using internal and external focus points.

- The best breathing techniques that you can use during labor.

- Relaxation techniques and even massage that can be used during the birth.

- Different ways that you can try to position yourself when you are going through birth and labor to make things easier.

- Normal labor, birth, and postpartum care.

The Bradley Method

This method is known as the husband coached birth. It is a method that will help a mother deliver without the use of pain medications and can prepare the father of the baby to be the birch coach of the mom. Although this method is mostly meant to help prepare a mother to give birth without any medications, it could also help you be prepared for any situations that come up and that you are not expecting, such as needing an emergency c-section.

This is a course that will take place over twelve sessions. In these sessions, you will learn:

- How important exercise and nutrition are during pregnancy

- Some different relaxation techniques that you can do for pain management

- Practicing for labor.

- How to avoid a c-section birth unless necessary.

- Postpartum care of the mother

- Breastfeeding

- Guidance for a coach for how to support the mother.

The Alexander Technique

This is a technique that is meant to improve the ease and freedom of coordination, flexibility, balance, and movement. You will ideally try to take these lessons each week while you are pregnant because it is more of an education process. The more that you practice this, the greater the benefits. Although this is a technique that can be useful for everyone, the goals for mothers who try this method are:

- To ease some of the discomforts that can come from nursing.

- Aid in recovering after giving birth

- An increase in how effective they are at pushing during the delivery

- An improved level of comfort during the pregnancy

Hypnobirthing

This is known as a Mangan method. This is a relaxed and natural childbirth education approach. This method is going to teach the mother how to use some self-hypnosis techniques to make it easier to handle labor. Teachers are going to spend time emphasizing childbirth and pregnancy, as well as on pre-birth parenting. This series is going to be five classes that are about two and a half hours long each.

These are just a few of the different child birthing classes that you can consider using. Each mother is different and you need to pick out the method that works the best for you.

Consider Baby CPR

You may want to consider doing a class that has information on baby CPR. You never know when your little one may get something stuck in their mouth or have trouble with breathing. Being certified in baby CPR can help give you the peace of mind of knowing that your baby will be safe at all times.

Permanent damage to the brain and even death could occur if the baby isn't able to breathe and blood flow stops. This is why every parent who is in charge of taking care of their child or an infant should know how to do this kind of CPR. There are classes in most areas, so looking at the website www.heart.org to find out where the classes are to you.

Many times, one of the other birthing classes that you pick will include some of these baby CPR classes as well. See if this is true for yours. If not, consider taking some time to become certified to make sure that you can always take care of your baby, even if the worst happens.

Do I Want to Do Cord Blood Banking?

Another thing that you may want to consider when you are getting ready for the hospital is to decide whether you want to do cord blood banking. Cord blood is the blood that is going to stay on the umbilical cord and the placenta after the birth. Most births discard this blood. However, you can use cord blood banking to help store and preserve the cord blood from your baby. If you are looking to do this, you must make sure that you work with a blood bank that is accredited by the AABB, or American Association of Blood Banks.

The cord blood is an important source of stem cells, ones that are specifically related through genetics to your baby and the rest of your family. These stem cells are considered dominant in the way that they can help systems, organs, and tissues develop in the body.

Stem cells are able to help transform some of the other cell types in the body in order to get them to create new growth and development. They are also important parts of the immune system. The transformation of these stem cells will help provide doctors with a way to treat some health disorders that are inherited and even treat leukemia.

The stem cells from this cord blood could be effective. Not only could it help with treating certain conditions for the baby, but also for siblings and parents. These blood stem cells have a similar ability to help treat the disease as bone marrow currently does, but there is actually less risk from rejection. Basically, this is a type of insurance against future disease, either in your baby or in someone else in your family. Hopefully, you would never run into a medical situation that would need these stem cells. But it can bring some peace of mind knowing that this resource is available if it is needed.

Once the cord blood is collected after the baby is born (make sure your doctor knows you want to do this so they don't discard the blood before you can get it), the blood is going to be processed before being stored in a laboratory facility, known as a blood bank. You can choose the blood bank you want to use, just make sure they have the right accreditation.

The collection of the cord blood has no indication of health risk which is good news. Since the retrieval is done after the cord has been cut, there shouldn't be any harm, discomfort, or pain. This helps to make the process as safe as possible.

The costs that you incur when you do this will depend on the bank that you choose to go with. There are often two fees that are involved in this kind of banking. The first is going to be the initial fee that will cover your enrollment, the collection, and then the storage for about the first year of this process. The second is going to be the storage fee that you pay for each year.

Depending on how much storage time is included in the initial amount, the fee that you pay in the beginning will range from $900 to $2100. Annual storage fees, after this time, will be about $100. It is common for many storage facilities to offer some prepaid plants at a discount, and some payment plans, so that you are more willing to store with them.

Deciding to do cord blood banking is a completely personal choice. Some parents know that they have a family history of some illnesses and diseases, so they choose to do this kind of treatment. Others decide they want to do it for peace of mind. It is a good idea to have a discussion about this before the birth to determine what you want to do.

Chapter 9:
Getting Ready for Labor: Stages of Labor

Your child's birth, whether it is your first child or your fourth, is a special experience. All deliveries are different and unique and there's no telling how yours will go. But no matter what, there are stages of each labor process, and knowing about them and what to expect can make a big difference in how you prepare.

Childbirth is going to occur through three stages. The first stage is the time when true labor starts. It continues going until the cervix has dilated all the way to 10 centimeters. The second stage is going to be the period of time after the cervix has dilated to the ten centimeters until the baby is delivered and in your arms. And the third stage is when the placenta is delivered. Let's take a look at each stage of labor and explore what happens in each one.

The First Stage of Labor
The longest stage of your labor is the first stage. This is pretty much everything that happens from the first real labor contraction that you feel all the way until you are ready to start pushing the baby out. It will have three phases that occur during it including:

- Early labor: This is the time when the first contraction occurs until the cervix reaches 3 centimeters.

- Active labor phase: This is going to be the phase that goes from three centimeters until the cervix reaches seven centimeters.

- Transition phase: This goes all the way until the cervix reaches full dilation.

Each phase is different and distinct. And the mother is going to find that there are different challenges, both physical and emotional, that they will deal with.

Early Labor Phase

During this phase, it is important to relax as much as possible. While the contractions may be painful and hard, this stage doesn't need to send you to the hospital or to your birthing center. Try to stay home and enjoy the comfort of your familiar surroundings, rather than getting straight to the hospital. If your early labor does occur during the day, try to lay back and take it easy, or even do a few simple routines in the house if you can.

The goal here is to keep yourself occupied while still conserving your energy as much as possible. For some women, this phase can progress quickly. But it is also possible for you to stay in this type of labor for many hours. The contractions are noticeable and may cause some pain, but you should still be able to move around and talk and do some regular activities.

During this time, make sure to eat some small snacks and drink water so that you can keep your energy up. Keep track of your contractions and time them so you have a basis point to refer to later when they get worse. If it is night time, and you are able to, try to get some sleep to help with your energy levels. If you can't fall asleep (and it is fine if you can't) concentrate on doing some small activities, such as packing your bag, doing a few dishes, or something else to distract yourself.

Some of the things that you can expect when you are in this early phase of labor include:

This type of labor will last about eight to twelve hours. This amount can change. Some women may get through this phase in a few hours though, so listen to your body and see if the contractions are getting worse. But until that happens, it is fine to sit back and relax or do some light chores around the house.

- During this phase, your cervix is going to efface and dilate out to three centimeters.

- Your contractions will usually last between thirty to 45 seconds each, and you will get somewhere between five to thirty minutes in between them.

- The contractions that you feel are usually going to be mild and, in the beginning, they will be irregular. But they will get stronger and more frequent as the labor progresses.

Contractions can feel different for everyone. Sometimes, they will feel like menstrual cramps. Sometimes, they will be a pain in your lower back, and sometimes, they will be a tightening or a pressure in the area of the pelvis.

Amniotic sac rupture may happen during this first stage of labor wherein your water breaks. Some people notice that their water breaks right at the beginning, but it isn't uncommon for it to break much later on when you are at the hospital.

When you are experiencing contractions, you need to pay attention to them. Notice if they are growing more intense as time goes on, if they are lasting longer or getting closer together, or if they seem to be following a regular pattern at all. And if the water does break, notice the odor and the color of the fluid. Also, keep track of the time it breaks because if too much time passes between the water breaking and the baby being born, it can increase the risk for infections.

If you have a support person around, whether it is a family member your spouse, or someone like a doula, there are a few things that they can do to help out as well. These include:

- The support person should keep up their strength as well. They need to be there to help the delivery and this requires energy as well.

- The support person can suggest some simple activities that can help to draw the focus of the mom away from the labor.

- The support person can offer support, reassurance, and comfort to mom.

- The support person should try to be a calming influence to the mom.

Work on timing the contractions. The mom is probably not going to remember to time these contractions, but that is important to the process. The support person can help with that.

Active Labor Phase

When you reach the active labor phase, it is time to head into the birth center or to the hospital. Your contractions during this stage are going to be longer, stronger, and much closer together. If possible, you will need to surround yourself with a lot of support. This is also the time when you will want to start some of the breathing techniques, and the relaxation exercises, between your contractions.

While you are at the hospital, you will want to make sure that you can switch your positions often during this phase. This can make the contractions easier to manage and can ensure that the labor goes faster. You can try to take a warm bath, try sitting in a different position, and even walking to help. Continue to drink plenty of water during this phase if the hospital allows it.

- There are a few things that you can expect during this phase. These things include:

- Your active labor is going to last about three to five hours.

- During this time, the cervix is going to dilate from four to seven centimeters.

- The contractions are going to get longer and closer. They will usually last between 45 to 60 seconds with up to five minutes of rest in between them.

- The contractions are going to feel a lot stronger.

- You can consider calling your doctor to make sure, but this is usually the time to head into the hospital.

Transition Labor Phase

The support person will most likely be relied on heavily by the mother during this phase. This phase is very challenging to get through, even though it is the shortest of the three. As the mother, try to use your breathing exercises and remember that you only have to get through one contraction at a time. If the contractions are close together, this is sometimes hard to do. But remember how far you have already come. When you start to feel the urge to push, it is time to get the baby out, and you should tell your healthcare provider right away.

This is a fast-paced phase of labor, and it is the last one before the baby is born. There are a few things that you can expect from this phase including:

- This phase is going to last somewhere between half an hour to two hours.

- Your cervix is going to dilate from 8 to 10 centimeters.

- The contractions during this phase are going to increase. They will usually last between 60 to 90 seconds, and there will be somewhere between a 30 second to 2-minute rest between each one.

- At this time, the contractions are going to be intense, strong, and long. And depending on how far along you are in this stage, they can even overlap.

- It is most often the hardest phase; however, the good news is that it can be the shortest.

- Each woman is different, but you may also experience side effects such as gas, vomiting, nausea, chills, or hot flashes during this time.

The Second Stage of Pregnancy

Once you go through the first stage of labor and have been dealing with the contractions for some time, it is time to move on to the second stage of labor. This is the time when you feel your body automatically trying to push the baby out, even without your help, and the doctor has said you are at ten centimeters. The second stage is going to involve all the pushing and then the delivery of the baby. Up to this point, the hormones in the body have made it possible to get to this point. But now you are going to have to step up and help out a little with pushing.

What Can I Expect When Pushing?
Many women who haven't gone through labor before may be curious what the pushing phase is like. Some of the things that you can expect during this phase of labor include:

- The pushing phase can expect anywhere from twenty minutes to two hours.

- The contractions are going to last between 45 to 90 seconds with three to five minutes in between.

- You will feel a strong natural urge to push. Pushing when you feel that urge can really help to expedite the process.

- You may feel a strong pressure at the rectum and some women will have a urination or minor bowel accident because of the pressure.

- After some time of pushing, the head of the baby is going to crown or become visible.

- You may feel a burning or stinging sensation during this crowning process, but each woman is different.

- During the crowning, your doctor is going to ask you not to push. Try to resist the urge to push here.

Try to find a position where you can have an advantage using gravity when you are pushing. Then, just push when you feel the urge. When you are in between the contractions, try to rest as much as possible to help get back some of your strength, or at least preserve it a little bit. If you want to, it is sometimes recommended to use a mirror so you can view your progress and get some encouragement when you see how far you have come. When it is time to push, don't hold back and use as much energy as you can to push.

One neat thing to know is that when you are in labor, your child is actually getting himself prepares to enter the outside world. They are an active participant and as long as everything goes well, they will also take steps to make sure that they can enter the world correctly. Some of the things that you will see your baby doing during this phase include:

- The head of the baby is going to turn over to one side and then the chin is going to rest on the chest automatically. This allows the back of the head to lead the way, which makes things easier.

- Once your body has had time to dilate fully, the head of the baby is going to lead the way. Then the torso and the head will begin to turn towards your back as they get down to the vagina.

- From here, the baby's head will start to emerge or crown through your vaginal opening.

- Once the baby's head is out, then the head and shoulders will turn to face your side to make it easier for the baby just to slip out.

What to Expect with Delivery?

Some women are not sure what to expect when they give birth for the first time. One thing to keep in mind is that when you do deliver, your baby has been soaking in the placenta, and in amniotic fluid, for the past nine months. Following all your contractions and a passage through your narrow birth canal, there may be some characteristics of the baby that are perfectly normal, but which you were not prepared for. Some of these include:

- Enlarged genitals

- Lanugo. This is a fine downy hair that is going to cover up the temple, forehead, back, and shoulders of the baby.

- Puffy eyes

- A vernix coating: This is a cheese-looking substance that can coat the fetus in the uterus.

- A head that is cone shaped.

The Third Stage of Labor: Delivering the Placenta

After the birth of your child, there is actually another stage of labor to go through. This third stage is the placenta's delivery. It is the stage where you will deliver the shortest and will only spend five to thirty minutes in total.

After your baby is delivered, your health care provider is going to be watching to see if there are any small contractions that occur with you again. These contractions signal that the placenta is separating from the uterine wall and that it is ready to be delivered.

It is also possible that a massage is done to apply pressure or the umbilical cord be gently pulled by the healthcare professionals. This results in the delivery of your placenta. Some mothers experience severe shivering and shaking after this happens, and this is completely normal and not something to be concerned about.

For the next few hours you may be monitored after you complete all of these stages of childbirth. This is to make sure that your uterus keeps contracting to heal and that the bleeding doesn't become excessive.

What Happens During A C-Section?

The birth that we described above is for a vaginal delivery. It can be done with or without medication to help the mother get through the pain. But there are times when you will need to have a c-section. Sometimes these are planned, such as when the mother has a complication when the baby needs to be delivered early, when the baby is in distress during labor, or when the mother is carrying more than one baby. Understanding what to expect during a pregnancy, whether it is a planned c-section or not, can make a difference in how you recover after the c-section is done.

With a c-section, your doctor is going to start out by explaining why they think it is necessary to perform cesarean section. A form of consent will be required to be signed by you. An obstetrician/midwife that can do the surgery will be assigned to you.

In most cases, your partner or husband can be with you during the preparation and during the birth. Sometimes the c-section, will be an emergency and there won't be time for your partner to change, they may not be allowed to stay in the operating room with you.

The anesthesiologist will then come in, if it is not an emergency, to review some of the pain management options that you can go with. It is never very common to be given general anesthesia anymore, except in an extreme situation. Usually, you are just given something for regional pain relief, like a spinal block or epidural. This helps you to have your lower half numb, but you will still be alert for when your baby is born.

If you had an epidural to help with pain relief during labor, you will also use the same pain relief during your cesarean section. Before the surgery, the doctor will give you some extra medication to ensure that you won't feel much during the surgery. Sometimes, you will feel a bit of tugging during the surgery, but there shouldn't be any pain. In this procedure, the urine is drained out from the urethra using a catheter. They will start the IV next to help with fluids and medications. You will then be moved over to the operating room.

During the procedure, you will be given antibiotics as well to help prevent any infections after the operation. The doctors will then administer the anesthesia and raise a screen so you won't see the surgery they make. You can choose to see the baby if you would like, just ask the nurse to lower the screen to see the baby.

Once your anesthesia has taken effect, the belly is going to have some antiseptic put on it. The doctor is then going to make a small horizontal incision above your pubic bone. They will then cut through all the underlying tissue, working their way down to the uterus. When the doctor reaches the abdominal muscles, they will manually separate them and spread apart to show the uterus underneath. The doctor can then reach in and pull out the baby. Once they have time to cut the cord, you will have a moment to see the baby before they hand them off to the nurse or the pediatrician. While the staff takes some time to examine the baby, the doctor is going to deliver the placenta and will then close up the incisions they made.

After taking some time to examine the baby, the nurse will hand them to your partner, who then has the option to hold them next to you. You can nuzzle, kiss, and talk to your baby while the doctor finishes stitching you up.

Over time, the stitches that are used to close up the incision will dissolve. The final layer may be closed up with staples or stitches, which will be removed three to seven days later. Sometimes, the doctor will use stitches that can dissolve. After the surgery is done, you will be moved over to the recovery room where you will be watched for the next few hours. If the baby is doing fine, they will be in the room with you and you can hold them. You will have to keep the IV in to help with eating and drinking.

At this time, if you plan to breastfeed, then this is the time to do it. You may find that nursing is the most comfortable for you and for the baby if you lie on your sides facing each other. Those who have c-sections are going to stay in the hospital for three days unless there are other complications. Your doctor will discuss your pain medication with you and how to treat your surgery after you go home.

Many mothers may not be prepared for a c-section. This can really change up their birthing plans, and they may be confused as to what is going on. C-sections are generally safe, especially if the baby made it to full term. You will just need to spend more time recovering. Most women who have c-sections will need to take about six weeks before they are feeling better and able to do the regular exercise again.

Heidi Oster

Chapter 10:
In-Hospital Procedures Commonly Done on a Newborn

After your baby is born, you may be curious about what is going to happen now. Many practitioners are going to allow you to hold onto the baby right after they are born. Warm towels or some blankets will be placed over you and the baby in order to make sure that the baby is warm. This is an important time for bonding and many birth centers and hospitals will give you that time before they do any other tests. Then, when you or the baby are both ready, there are some tests that all hospitals will go through.

This newborn testing is very important and it is something that you should think about before the birth. During pregnancy, we are going to focus so much on the actual birth that sometimes we may not even think about this newborn testing. There are several different tests that will be done at your hospital, and some of the most common ones include:

Measuring the Length and Weight
The timing of these tests can vary based on your hospital, but they will be done at some point during the first few hours of your baby's life. Some hospitals will do it after a few minutes of skin-to-skin contact, and others will wait. Most professionals believe that this is a bad thing because the bonding period is so important. The baby only has a short amount of time when they

are alert after birth and many professionals believe they should use this time to bond with the parents.

Many parents are now writing out their birth plans so that the procedures for these tests are put off until later. They usually try to delay this for the first hour or so after the baby is born. You can talk to your doctor to see what their rules are for your hospital and if there is any room to move the timing of this.

Doing Eye Drops

Eye drops have changed in many states recently. In the past, Silver Nitrate was used in most hospitals. This would burn the baby's eyes a bit, but it was used to help prevent an infection. It is now becoming more common for hospitals to use erythromycin instead. Make sure that you talk to your doctor to see which one is being used.

While the eye drops are important to help prevent infections in the baby, it is still another thing that you can delay until later on. Most states say that it is up to your doctor to put the eye drops in, but there isn't a time indicated there. This means that you and your doctor can decide when to put these drops in. As long as you get these done in the first few hours, it will be fine.

A Vitamin K Injection

This is another injection that the baby will need to get after birth. Babies are not going to be born with a good clotting system. This is where the vitamin K injection came into place. This became law when force deliveries were common in order to prevent any bleeding in the brain due to trauma that this procedure could cause to the head.

Today, it is still common to give the vitamin K injection, despite the fact that most deliveries are not done with the forceps any longer. This is because vitamin K can provide some good benefits to the baby. Some countries have different policies on when to provide this injection rather than doing it all of the time. This injection is something that you should consider talking with your doctor to figure out what will work the best for you.

Newborn Screening and PKU Testing

Newborn screening is a term that is used to define the whole set of tests that is done in order to screen your baby for a variety of diseases, including PKU. While many moms state that they are having this PKU screening, it is common that the newborn screening is going to be done for many disorders all at the same time. The tests that are done will vary depending on the state.

The newborn screening is going to involve sticking the foot of your baby for blood. This test is only going to be accurate when the baby has received a diet that contains phenylalanine, which can come from artificial formulas and milk, for at least 24 hours. This is why a baby is breastfed until at least one day after they are born. Taking it earlier than this could give you results that are not accurate.

Hepatitis Vaccine Administration

This is now a vaccine that most states will require you to have. You will have two choices for when you can start this vaccine though. You can either give it to your child when they are first born, or you can do it when you have their two-month check-up. You should first look at your own risk for developing hepatitis and then decide on the best time to give it to your child.

Apgar Testing

This test is technically the first test that your baby will get. In most places, it is done in the first few moments that the baby is born before they even hand the baby over to you. Often, the parents don't know that it happened. This test is simply an evaluation of the way that the baby sounds and looks when they are first born.

The medical professional is going to give a score for each sign at one minute and at five minutes after birth. If there seem to be any issues with the baby, an additional score can be given at ten minutes. A score that is between seven and ten is normal, four to seven might need some help from the doctor, and if the score is at three or below, it means that the baby needs immediate medical attention.

Remember, this score does not correspond with the intelligence levels, or the SAT score, that your child will have later in life. In some circles, this test is seen as not very useful. For example, a baby who needs help or who is in distress is not going to wait or be left alone until the doctor performs the APGAR at one minute. This is a harmless test, but many doctors are going to choose other methods to help watch the baby.

Depending on the type of pregnancy you had and how the baby is doing, there may be other tests that your doctor will want to perform. They may want to do blood sugar testing, hearing tests, and more. Make sure to talk to your doctor about the tests that they wish to complete so you are fully informed about what will happen after delivery.

Chapter 11:
Post Recovery

After your baby is born, there is a lot that you need to keep track of. During this time, you are getting used to your changing body, to the new baby, and even to some physical pains. If you had a c-section, the time can take even longer before you feel better. As a new mother, you need to take some special care of your body after giving birth, and while breastfeeding as well. Doing this will help you to regain your energy and your strength. Let's take a look at some of the steps that you can take to help recover from birth.

Getting Your Rest

After you have been released from the hospital (one to three days for vaginal delivery and three to five days for a c-section as long as there aren't any complications), you should spend the first few days relaxing as much as possible. You need to focus your energy on yourself and spend this time getting familiar with your baby.

Even though there are probably a ton of excited requests from family and friends to come over and meet the baby, try to limit your visitors so that you can get as much rest as you can. Do not put a lot of unnecessary expectations on yourself. For example, you do not need to keep your house sparkling clean. During that first bit of time at home, you may only be able to sleep, eat, and take care of your baby, and there is nothing wrong with that. Try to lie down and sleep when the baby sleeps. Don't worry about cleaning the house. And if others offer, allow them to help out when they can.

Physical Changes

After your baby is born, your doctor will spend some time talking to you about some of the changes that you will go through as your body works at recovering. Some of the things you may notice include:

- There may be some swelling in the feet and legs. The best way to deal with this is to keep your feet elevated when you can.

- There is the possibility that you will feel constipated. Some fresh produce and plenty of water can help with this.

It is common to feel some menstrual like cramping, especially for those who are breastfeeding. Your milk will come in sometime between three and six weeks after delivery. Even if you are not breastfeeding, you may have some milk leaking and your breasts could feel uncomfortable, full, or tender.

Follow the instructions your doctor gives for how much activity such as walking, doing chores, and more, that you are allowed to do.

During your postpartum visit, which occurs about six weeks after birth, your doctor will check in on your recovery. You can take that time to ask about resuming some of your normal activities. Ask about the right fitness and eating plans to help you get back to a healthy weight over time.

You should also take this time to talk about sex and birth control with your doctor unless you would like to have two kids right on top of each other. It is possible that your period would return within six to eight weeks, or even sooner if you don't breastfeed. For some women who breastfeed, your period may not come back for many months. The best way to prevent a pregnancy until you are ready is to find a reliable form of birth control.

Regaining A Healthy Weight

Both the pregnancy and the labor you go through at the end will have an effect on your body. After you give birth, it is likely that you will lose around ten pounds right away because of the weight of the baby, the placenta, and the fluids that you lost as well. It is not a good idea to try and lose any additional pregnancy weight right away. Slow weight loss over several months is the best method, especially if you plan to breastfeed. Mothers who are nursing can safely lose a moderate amount of weight without any worries about how their milk supply will be influenced.

A healthy eating plan and some regular exercise might be enough for some women to return to their healthy weight. If you find that you aren't really losing weight, or it is taking too long, make sure that you cut back on foods that have extra sugars and fats, soft drinks, desserts, and so on. When you focus your energy on a well-balanced diet, you can help yourself lose weight while also giving yourself and your baby the nutrition you need.

Feeling Blue

After you give birth, it is normal to feel sad, weepy, and overwhelmed for a few days. This is pretty common due to the changing hormones, some anxiety about how to care for the baby, and a general lack of sleep because you have a newborn. All of these are normal, and it is important to be patient with yourself here. They will usually go away quickly. But if you notice that your sadness is lasting more than two weeks, you should go see your doctor. Even if it is before your postpartum visit, go ahead and do this.

You could be dealing with a serious, but very treatable condition known as postpartum depression. It is possible that postpartum depression can happen at any time within your first year after giving birth. Some of the signs that you will notice with postpartum depression include:

- Thoughts about harming either yourself or your baby

- Having no interest or not getting any pleasure from various activities such as socializing or sex.

- Feeling guilty or worthless

- Not having much interest in your baby

- Being worried all the time about the baby

- Trouble with focusing, remembering things, or making any decisions

- Overeating and weight gain

- Not being able to eat and then losing weight

- Having trouble with sleeping, being tired, or a combination of both.

- Having chest pains, headaches, heart palpitations, hyperventilation or numbness

- No energy at all.

- Crying often, feeling depressed or sad.

- Feeling irritable or restless.

Some women are not going to talk about the symptoms they are feeling because they may feel guilty or embarrassed about them. Don't let this happen to you. This kind of depression can make it hard for some women to take care of their baby, and it could lead to issues with emotional bonding and developmental milestones in your baby. Your doctor can help you to feel better and can get you back to enjoying the baby. Medicine and or therapy can help to treat this kind of depression.

Heidi Oster

Chapter 12: FAQ's

What Is the Best Sleeping Position When You Are Pregnant?

The best position to sleep in is one that will keep the curve of your back in line. Sleeping on your side with one of the knees bent can work nicely. Just make sure that you aren't lying with the knees all the way up to your chest. During the third trimester, it is best to avoid lying on your back because it will make the heart work more and can cause a big backache. Lying on your stomach during this time may not be comfortable and it can add pressure to the fetus. Use a pillow under the head, but not on your shoulders. Some women find that having a pillow between their legs can help as well.

What Are Some of The Early Symptoms of Pregnancy?

Outside of a missed period, there are some other symptoms that you may notice when you are pregnant. Pregnancy can bring about changes in your hormonal balance, and this could include a variety of symptoms like:

- Frequent urination
- Constipation
- Mood swings
- Headaches

- Fainting and dizziness

Why Do I Have So Many Cravings When I Am Pregnant?

Some women will find that they have strong cravings, or they can't stand certain foods once they become pregnant. This is related to all the hormonal changes that occur during this time. This effect is often so strong that some women will find that their stomachs just can't stand some of the foods that used to be their favorites.

How Long Do the Cravings and Nausea Last During Pregnancy?

It is possible for some women that the food aversions, cravings, and nausea will last for your whole pregnancy. But for most women, these symptoms are going to lessen between the 13th and 14th week of the pregnancy. Until that happens, it is important to eat a diet that is as healthy as possible to ensure that your baby can get the essential nutrients they need. If you are having trouble eating because of nausea, then it is important to talk to your doctor about this.

What Nutrients Should I Look for Inside My Prenatal Vitamins?

Some of the nutrients, and their amounts, that you should aim for in your prenatal vitamin include:

- 150 micrograms of iodine
- 17 mg iron
- 15 mg zinc
- 10 mg vitamin E

- 6 mcg vitamin B12
- 20 mg niacin
- 2 mg riboflavin
- 3 mg thiamine
- 70 mg vitamin C
- 200 or more mg calcium
- 400 IU vitamin D
- 400 mcg folic acid

What Is the Difference Between Effaced and Dilated?

Effaced means how thinned out the cervix is and dilated is how opened up it is. You need to have the cervix effaced to 100 percent and then it needs to be dilated to 10 centimeters before you are able to deliver your baby.

What Are the Benefits of Breastfeeding My Baby?

There are a number of benefits your baby can enjoy when you breastfeed, and it is even beneficial to mom too! Some of the benefits of breastfeeding your baby includes:

- It can provide some antibodies that will help your baby resist illness
- It is easier to digest compared to formula. This means the baby will be less gassy and constipated.
- It can help to reduce the risk of SIDS in your baby.

- Some studies find that babies who were breastfed may have higher levels of cognitive function.

- Breast milk may be able to help your baby fight against lymphoma, leukemia, high cholesterol, and diabetes.

Do I Need to Make Changes in My Diet If I Have Diabetes?

If you find out you have diabetes during your pregnancy, or you had diabetes as a pre-existing condition before your pregnancy, then you may need to work with your doctor to adjust your diet. Changing your diabetes diet while you are pregnant can help you avoid some issues with high or low blood sugar levels.

How Does My Doctor Figure Out When My Pregnancy Started?

Most of the time, it is hard to know the exact day that you got pregnant. The doctor will usually count your pregnancy start from the first day of the last menstrual period. This is often about two weeks ahead of when conception occurred.

Are Prescription Drugs Harmful to My Baby While I'm Pregnant

Some medications can be harmful to the baby when you are pregnant. If you are on any medications, you should talk to your doctor about those medications and if they are still safe to take while you are pregnant. If you develop an issue during the pregnancy, your doctor will decide if a prescription medication is the best option for you, or if you should go with something else.

Why Would I Need to Have My Labor Induced?

There are several reasons why your doctor may decide to induce your pregnancy. Some of these include:

- You are past your due date by one or two weeks. The longer you go past your due date, the higher the risk you will have for complications.

- Your water breaks, but labor doesn't start. Once the water breaks, you and the baby could get an infection.

- You have some other health problem that could put the baby at risk. Issues like preeclampsia, high blood pressure, and diabetes could make it so you will want to induce water.

- A test that your doctor did may show that the baby has a problem. If the baby isn't growing right or they have an abnormal heart rate, the doctor may decide to induce you.

What Happens During My Oral Glucose Tolerance Test?

This test is going to involve the mother quickly drinking a special sweetened liquid. This drink has about 50g of glucose. The body is able to absorb this glucose quickly, which can cause your levels of blood glucose to rise within an hour. Then you will give a blood sample to measure how the glucose was stored by the body. It can help indicate if you have gestational diabetes.

Can I Exercise While I Am Pregnant?

Yes, it is fine to exercise while you are pregnant. In most cases, it is fine to exercise at the levels that you did before your pregnancy. Just make sure you are comfortable and that you have approval from your doctor.

What Are Some of The Advantages of Genetic Testing?

One benefit of doing genetic testing is to find out any problems that may be unknown before this. Many flawed genes that these tests are able to find won't be linked to your family history, ethnicity, or race. You may not have known that you or your partner carry these issues and knowing the risk can help you make some better decisions about your family.

These tests can also provide you with some answers about your family history. The results have shown many families if they are in a high-risk group. The test is easy to do because you simply take a saliva or blood sample before you are pregnant and it is harmless and quick to do.

What Are Braxton Hicks Contractions?

Many women are going to have a harmless false labor pain known as Braxton Hicks contractions. These are pretty erratic, and they are not going to get closer together. They often stop when you either rest or move around. These are not considered a part of the level. If you are not sure about which types of contractions you are dealing with, then you should get medical help.

Conclusion

Thank you for making it through to the end of *What to Expect for First Time Moms*. Let's hope it was informative and able to provide you with all of the tools you need to achieve your goals whatever they may be.

The next step is to use this guidebook to help you get through the different parts of your pregnancy. Pregnancy is an exciting time, but many new expectant mothers aren't sure about what is going to happen at each stage of their pregnancy. This guidebook is meant to provide you with the information that you need, whether you want to know how to pick out a doctor, what happens during each week of the pregnancy, or even what to expect during labor and beyond.

If you find this book helpful in anyway a review to support my endeavors is much appreciated.

Baby Sleep Guide to Promote Healthy Sleep Habits

Wise Tips and Tricks to Help Your Newborn Sleep Through the Night, Proven Modern Training to Calm Crying Infants for No Cry Nights and a Happy Child

Heidi Oster

Introduction

The following chapters will discuss everything that you need to know to help get your baby to sleep at night. There are many parents who are ready to get their baby to fall asleep at night. Sure, they love the cuddles and all the relaxing time with their baby, but they don't like having the baby attached to them all the time. They want to be able to do things around the house, take a bath, or even get to bed without having an upset baby every night of the week.

This guidebook is going to discuss some of the different sleep training methods that you can use to help put your baby to sleep at night. Some will require a bit of assistance from the parent and others follow the cry it out method to help baby get to sleep at night. Each of these methods can be effective; you just need to find the one that works the best for you and for your baby.

In addition to discussing the different sleep training methods that are inside this guidebook (even though that is the meat and potatoes and the main reason you are here), we will discuss some of the other things you need to know about your baby and how they sleep. We will look at some of the different guidelines for how babies sleep at different ages; some great tools that can help you get the baby to sleep and keep them asleep, and even some of the common problems you may encounter when you try to sleep train.

Heidi Oster

Every parent loves their baby, but they also love to sleep as well. Use this guidebook to help you get that baby to sleep safely and independently.

Chapter 1:
What You Need to Know About Baby Sleep

Having a new baby can be an exciting time. You went through the whole pregnancy excited to have the baby, and now that you have that little bundle of joy and have learned their little personalities, you are on cloud nine. But now that you are taking care of your new baby and perhaps their siblings as well, you are tired and worn out. And if your baby has trouble falling asleep at night, then this can make the exhaustion even worse.

This book is meant to help out parents who have a challenging baby or child who just won't go to sleep. This can be children who have their days and nights mixed up, the ones who will only sleep when they are in their parent's arms, or those who just have trouble sleeping altogether. Let's take a look at some of the things that you need to know to get started with baby sleep training and help you to finally get the baby to sleep through the night.

Things I Need to Know to Start
Before we get in-depth about sleep training and how to do it on your baby, there are a few truths that we need to know about. These truths are going to be fundamental to helping us know what is going to happen when we start on sleep training. There are often a lot of misunderstandings about sleep training, so having these out of the way can make sleep training so much easier.

You are the best parent to your child. Yes, parenting can be hard, and at times, when the child is awake in the middle of the night, you may feel like a failure. Just remember that you aren't a failure. You are amazing. No one can do better for your child than you, and your child is so lucky that you are their parent.

You and your partner will probably get into many fights about your child and how well they sleep. This is just something that happens when you get tired and frustrated. You may have one night where you are whisper-fighting at three in the morning about how you should handle the crying baby. And the next night you will think that your husband is a jerk because they are pretending to sleep in order to deal with whatever is happening with the baby. Everyone can get grumpy when they feel tired. Forgive each other during this time. Someday when the baby is grown up and sleeps through the night, you will laugh about the whole thing.

Babies are not going to outgrow sleep issues. Rather, they grow into them. You may as well get ready for a hard time now. If you get started with it today, this will help you to get sleep later. Your kid won't simply outgrow the sleep issues. They will just get worse unless you teach them the right sleep habits early on.

Remember that sometimes babies won't sleep the way that you want them to simply because they are babies. And for today, that is something that you need to accept because it's as good as it gets. Over time, things will get better so don't despair here.

Helping your child get some healthy sleep habits now is one of the best parenting decisions that you can do for them. As a new parent, there is probably a ton of noise around you about how to be a good parent and how to do this or that. But it all boils down to giving your child all the love you have to give, spend time with them each day, play with them outside, and help them to sleep. If you can handle these few tasks, then you are doing everything right for your child.

And while this guidebook does focus on sleep training, it is important to not become obsessed with the sleep pattern of your child. Sure, getting them on a sleep pattern is important for their health and their development. But if you spend all day, every day focusing on how you will get them to sleep and worrying about whether they are sleeping or not, you will miss out on all the fun stuff that comes with having a baby.

Learning how to get your baby to sleep at night is a process. It is not something that you will be able to do in one night. In fact, you need to be in for the long haul. There may be times when it gets harder before it gets better. But if you persist with the work, and realize that it will get better you will soon be able to get your baby to sleep through the night without all the hassles and all the roadblocks that you are facing now.

Where Should the Baby Sleep?

Hopefully, at this point, you have a plan for where you want to let the baby sleep. Newborns don't always go with the plan that you have in place, so remember that a little flexibility can be important. But have a firm idea and aim for it when the baby is about six months old or so. Some parents like to have the baby sleep well in a crib in their own room, and others may like them to sleep in the same room as the parent.

No matter what your long-term goal is, most babies end up sharing a room with their parents for at least a bit of their first few months. This often makes it easier for parents to hear their babies and can shorten the distance the parent has to travel when it is time to feed the baby. Keep in mind that room sharing and co-sleeping are not the same things.

Babies who spend at least the first few months in a room with their parents actually have a lower incidence of SIDS. This is why it is often recommended for babies between the newborn and six-month stage. And because newborns require quite a bit of night parenting, having the baby nearby can be really convenient for the parent as well.

If it is more convenient for you, or you and the baby will sleep better when the baby is in another room, that is fine as well. Some parents find that they do better when the baby is in their own room. If you are doing this, make sure that you have a crib prepared for the baby, one with tight-fitting sheets, no extra blankets, or toys inside, and that the baby lies down on their back.

The other decision that you will need to make is what kind of sleep-surface you want the baby to be on. Now, you may find that you have some ideas with this, but the baby prefers to go with something else. Let's say that for now, you get the choice and your baby will go wherever you put them!

According to the American Academy of Pediatrics, your baby should only ever sleep in a play yard, bassinet, or crib that meets the CPSC safety standards. However, many parents find that it is hard to get their newborn to sleep well in a crib when they first bring them home. While you should try to put the baby in a crib, some do well with this and may surprise you, and in some, you may find that it doesn't work that well.

Combining crib-sleeping and co-rooming can be a challenge. Most of the time you won't be able to get the crib through the doorway and you would have to take it apart when you are ready to move it. Space limitations in your bedroom can make this difficult as well. This can present a problem. You may want to talk with your pediatrician and see if you can find a safe sleep space that allows the child to sleep well and that can also be put int your room. Something like a portable crib may work best.

A Note About Co-Sleeping

The co-rooming that we have been talking about at this point is when the baby sleeps in the same room as you. Co-sleeping is when the baby sleeps with you in your bed. Sometimes co-sleeping is going to occur all night as a decision by the parent. And other times the baby will fall asleep in their crib (or another sleeping place), and then join the parents in bed as a last-ditch effort to finally get the baby to sleep in the middle of the night.

There are a lot of different options when it comes to co-sleeping. Some parents choose to co-sleep because they like the convenience, find that the baby sleeps better when nearby, or they like to have the baby physically near them all of the time. This is known as proactive co-sleeping and it will last for the full night. Some parents may choose to just do co-sleeping for naps to make things easier.

There is also reactive co-sleeping. This is when parents didn't want or plan to co-sleep, but when they find the baby won't sleep in another fashion, they resort to this. Or, they may have brought the baby in to breastfeed them and then the baby and the parent fell asleep.

Proactive co-sleeping is something that has brought up a lot of controversy in the United States, but it is a cultural phenomenon. Asian countries exclusively co-sleep with their infants, and sometimes with older children. In fact, up to 59 percent of Japanese parent's co-sleep with their babies. In the United States, this type of co-sleeping is less common and it is estimated that only about 9 percent of families do this.

Many doctors and health professionals recommend that you don't co-sleep with your baby, but there is a growing number of parents who are showing the benefits of co-sleeping and how it can help the parent and the baby develop a strong bond. If you are considering working with co-sleeping, do it only if you are drug-free, don't drink alcohol, and if you don't smoke. And make sure to discuss this matter with your doctor to see if this is a good idea for you and for your baby, and to learn any of the safety measures that you should follow to keep your baby safe during this time.

If you do decide to co-sleep with your baby, some of the rules that you should consider include:

- Do not co-sleep with a baby who is premature.

- Do not co-sleep with pets, other adults that are not the parents, or siblings.

- Parents who smoke should never co-sleep.

- Use a firm bed surface. This means no waterbeds, air beds, or mattress toppers, pillows, blankets, or thick bedding.

- Pull the bed away from the wall and then take the headboard off if you can to reduce any risks of the baby getting trapped between things.

- Never leave the baby alone on the adult bed. No matter how big the bed or small the child, they may be able to roll out sooner than you would think.

- If you can, consider putting the mattress right on the floor to reduce some of the risks.

Sleep Safety Rules

Before we get started on some of the sleeping techniques in this guidebook, it is important to talk about some of the safe sleeping rules. These ensure that once you get the baby to sleep, you are able to keep them safe during the night. Some of the rules that you want to consider include:

Place the Baby on Their Back for Sleeping

In the past, mothers were told that their babies should be placed to sleep on their front. This was because the thoughts at the time were that babies were less likely to choke when they were sick if they were in this position. But according to research that has been done throughout the world, the safest position for a baby is to be put down on their back.

This research has found that the risk of SIDS in your baby will increase six times if they are sleeping on their front. And since there is no rise in choking in babies who sleep on their back, this is a completely safe position for them to sleep in. When you place the baby down in their bed at night, make sure that you make sure they are on their back. If your baby does happen to roll over to their tummy during the night, just gently turn them back over again. After they turn six months old and are able to turn onto their tummies and then back again on their own, then it is fine to let your baby stay on their tummies if they happen to roll over at night.

Keep the Bed Clear for Your Baby

When you lay the baby down to sleep for the night, make sure that you don't have anything in the crib with this. Don't have any bulky or soft bedding, pillows, a cot bumper, duvets, quilts, or soft toys inside. All of these things can cause a suffocation risk, and with a bumper, there is also a strangulation risk involved as well. It is especially important to avoid using pillows in the crib because studies done by different groups, including the Lullaby Trust, show that a pillow alone could double the risk of SIDS for your baby.

Some of the things that you can do to help make sure the bedding around your baby is as safe as possible are the following:

- Take any blankets and sheets that you are using and tuck them in as firmly as possible. Place your baby with the feet at the foot of the bed so that they aren't able to wiggle down and get the sheets over their heads.

- Use a sleeping bag. These are going to keep the baby warm and will ensure that they won't need any blankets or sheets in the first place.

Remember that it is perfectly safe to swaddle your baby, as long as you make sure you do it properly. Don't swaddle above the shoulders and don't do the swaddle too tightly. Once the baby is able to roll over, when they reach about four months old, you should stop using this practice.

Don't Allow the Baby to Get Hot

While it is in our instincts to wrap up the baby as much as possible, letting the baby get too hot could increase the risks of SIDS. This is especially important to remember any time that it is cold outside. Babies actually need a cooler room than most people might assume. The recommended safe temperature for the baby at night is between 61 and 68 degrees.

You don't want to rely on just how the room feels to you. Make sure to use a room thermometer to make sure. You can also check on the baby to see if they are overheating. Don't check at the feet though because, like adults, the feet can often run much colder than the rest of the body. Look at the tummy or the back of the neck of your baby to see how warm they are.

Keep the House Smoke-Free

This is a safety parenting advice that will start during your pregnancy. There is a huge link between SIDS and parents who smoke. While there isn't definitive evidence out there for this, many groups believe that about 30 percent of sudden infant deaths could be avoided if the mothers didn't smoke when they were pregnant. The best advice that you can follow for this one includes:

- When you find out you are pregnant, make sure to stop smoking and have anyone else around you or around the house stop smoking as well.

- Don't allow anyone to smoke in the same room as the baby.

- Don't allow visitors to your house to smoke in the home. Some parents

- choose to ask visitors not to smoke at all, and some request them to smoke outside.

- Don't take the baby into places that are going to be smoky.

Never Sleep on An Armchair or The Sofa with Your Baby

While you may find at times that it is easy to fall asleep while holding the baby on your sofa, sleeping with the baby can be dangerous because it can increase the risk of SIDS. This is because the baby can slip into the gaps of the cushions of the couch, or the sofa back and the cushions. It is also possible for you to slip down or roll on top of the baby. Many deaths of babies happen because the parent and baby fall asleep on the sofa together.

If you are sitting on the sofa with your baby and feeding them and you are worried that you might fall asleep, then bring out the phone and set an alarm. This will wake you up within a few minutes if you do fall asleep. If you are sitting on the sofa and holding the baby, make sure to set them down in their baby-box, Moses basket, crib, or cot.

Share A Room with The Baby

During the first six months, it is safest for your baby to sleep in a crib or cot in whichever room you are in. According to a 2013 study that was funded by The Lullaby Trust, about 75 percent of the babies who died from SIDS during the day were sleeping in a room all on their own.

The reason that sleeping in the same room with the baby might be that having the parent nearby could have a type of protective effect on the baby. Or maybe having the baby near you allows you to respond to the needs of the baby better. Either way, room sharing with your baby definitely helps reduce the risks of SIDS.

Remember that room sharing and co-sleeping are not the same things. While room sharing is safe, co-sleeping can be unsafe for your baby. You can run the risk of issues with rolling over and on top of the baby while you are sleeping. It is best to let the baby sleep in the same room as you, but make sure they are in their own area to sleep, such as in a bassinet or a crib.

Heidi Oster

Chapter 2:
Bedtime Problems and How to Can Fix Them

As a new parent, there are a lot of things that you need to pay attention to when it comes to bedtime. You want to ensure that your baby is getting the amount of sleep that they need to be healthy and happy, but if you are struggling with some of the common bedtime problems that other new parents are, this process may be easier said than done. Here are a few of the most common bedtime problems you may be dealing with concerning your little one and the steps you can take to fix them.

The Bedtime Chosen Is Too Late

A late bedtime is one of the challenges that new parents may face. It is going to show up with bedtime battles, waking up often during the night, and an early start to the day. Think of this as "baby is awake too long before bedtime," which means that the baby is going to be overtired. Despite what many parents may think, an overtired baby will have a hard time falling and staying asleep.

If you are struggling with getting your child to fall asleep, it may be time to switch up their bedtime a bit. Even moving it ahead a few minutes each day until it gets to a more reasonable time can make a difference in how well the baby sleeps. If you had a child who fell asleep without any issues and now, they are struggling to sleep, you may have moved bedtime a little early. This is a balancing act and you may have to experiment to find the perfect bedtime for your baby.

The Bedtime Is Inconsistent

Some kids are going to have a bedtime that is really inconsistent. With newborns, you may find that you choose bedtimes based on how the naps went that day so you can make sure they get enough sleep. If the baby took short naps that day, you may move the bedtime to earlier to help them get enough sleep. If they took a long nap, you may let them stay up a little later.

But for kids who are older than 3 months, it is important to lock them into a consistent bedtime. Varying times of going to bed can make it harder for the baby to fall asleep. There have also been studies that show how an inconsistent bedtime can even be associated with a higher rate of a behavioral problem later on.

If your goal is to help your child sleep better at night, then you need to look at your schedule and make some adjustments to bedtime so that this happens as close to the same time as possible every day. Lock this in and keep it there.

The Bedtime Is Too Early for The Baby

Sometimes your baby may go to bed too early. Even though we just talked about the benefits of making sure your baby doesn't go to bed too late, it is still possible that you are picking out a bedtime that is too early. Some of the indicators that you are putting your baby to bed too early include:

- The baby consistently struggles to fall asleep at bedtime. Most babies and even older kids will be fast asleep within twenty minutes of going to bed.

- Your child is routinely awake and won't go back to sleep for longer periods of time in the middle of the night. Some babies will do this on occasion, but when it happens all the time, you may need to reconsider the bedtime.

- The bedtime doesn't have a long enough stretch of awake-time ahead of it. If the baby went down for a nap about an hour before bedtime, they probably won't be ready to go to bed for the night.

- Your child has a healthy amount of sleep, which is between ten to twelve hours at night but wakes up too early for you, then it may be time to push bedtime back an hour.

If you are getting a combination of these symptoms, then it may be time to make the bedtime a little later each night. Start by doing fifteen minutes later each day until you get to the bedtime that works the best for you. If you do this for seven nights in a row and you don't really see an improvement, then it is fine to go back to the original bedtime that you had.

Bedtime Stinks

Once your child is no longer a newborn, the bedtime in your home should be your favorite time of the day. You may enjoy all the cuddles, the cute pajamas, and the quiet that you are going to get when they go to sleep can be so welcome for many parents. But sometimes, figuring out what is causing your baby to stay awake and not fall asleep can evade you. There are many ways that bedtime can stink for a new parent including:

- It takes ages to soothe the baby and get them to sleep.

- You have to go back and forth into your baby's room a million times before they fall asleep.

- Your child is up so late most nights that you pretty much go to bed right after they do.

- Bedtime is a long stretch of limit-testing cries for more. This could be for more books, kisses, hugs, water, and so on.

If this sounds like something that happens at your home, then it is time to figure out why bedtime stinks so bad, and then come up with a good plan to help improve it. The plan that you use will depend on the reason that bedtime is so bad and how old the baby is at the time. The good news is that with some time and patience, and the right plan, you will soon get the baby to sleep through the night.

Chapter 3:
What Is Normal Sleeping Behavior

One of the best things that you can do to help with understanding your baby and the way that they sleep is to know how babies tend to sleep during the different stages of their lives. If you start with sleep training when the baby is too young, you are going to put in a lot of wasted effort. For example, a newborn is not going to get on a regular schedule, no matter how hard you try. But by the time they reach about nine months old, you can get them into a good sleeping pattern. Let's look at the sleep development of different age groups, as your baby gets older.

What Is Normal for A Newborn?
The newborn stage of sleeping is one of the toughest ones for new parents to get through. The baby is often on a sporadic sleep schedule and will not sleep for long periods of time. Newborns are going to sleep in short little bouts, usually ranging from half an hour to four hours, and there won't be much routine in the times they get this sleep. Their sleep time can vary quite a bit. During the first few days, they may sleep between sixteen and eighteen hours each day. By the time they get to four weeks, they average out to fourteen hours. But this can vary between babies as well. Some need more and some need less.

The time of when adults fall asleep is going to be controlled by their circadian rhythms. This is a physiological change that will follow a regular 24-hour cycle. Many of these can be influenced by how much light exposure we get. For instance, when you expose yourself to some sunlight throughout the day, you are helping the body calibrate its internal clock. Even if you are low on sleep, morning light can make sure that you are alert during the day.

On the other side of things, the absence of light is going to help the body slow down a bit. When darkness falls, your brain is going to interpret this as a signal to start producing melatonin, a hormone that can trigger the body to relax and can make it easier to fall asleep.

It is possible for you to disrupt this process a bit. For example, if you expose yourself to some artificial light sources throughout the evening, especially if they are blue lights, you may confuse the body. But as long as you stick with the program, having light during the day and dark at night, you will usually find your natural rhythm.

However, a newborn is not going to be governed by this strong circadian rhythm. It doesn't necessarily start out this way. In the womb, the newborn fell into the same patterns as the mother. The fetal breathing and heart rates would speed up when the mother was active and then slow down when the mother was sleeping. These changes could see some help from some of the hormones from the mother, especially melatonin.

But after birth, this hormonal connection is broken and it is up to the newborn to develop these circadian rhythms themselves. This is a process that takes time. The baby is not going to be born able to do this, and this can mean a lot of long nights for mom and dad. At about twelve weeks old, the baby will start to show the day and night rhythms due to the fact that they start producing melatonin. This is when they will start to get more of the regular sleep patterns that can help mom and dad get more sleep at night as well.

What Is Normal for Three to Six Months?

When you include the naps and nighttime sleeping, your three to six-month-old will sleep between fifteen and sixteen hours a day. Typically, by the time the baby reaches four months, they are going to develop some more regular patterns when it comes to being asleep and awake and some have been able to drop down to fewer night feedings at that time.

This doesn't mean that it is time to make a really rigid sleep program for your four-month-old. If your baby has developed some sleep patterns that are steady and fit in well with the schedule that you want, that is fine. Go ahead and encourage these a bit. But if you want to make sure that your baby is able to sleep longer at one time and have more regular hours, then this is a good time to introduce a bit of sleep training.

Remember that while there are some generalizations, each baby has their own unique developmental schedule. Observe how your child reacts to sleep training, and if they don't seem ready, then you can wait a bit and try it again in a few weeks. At some point though, somewhere between four and six months, most babies will be able to sleep through at least a few hours at a time. Once this happens, you will feel more relieved because you as the parent will be able to get in a few full sleep cycles as well.

Some babies who did well with sleeping through the night early on in this period may find that they go through a sleep regression or a period of time when they start waking up every few hours again. This is just temporary and will usually end, as long as you keep with your regular bedtime routine as much as possible. The baby may be growing, may be practicing some of their new skills in their sleep and waking up, or becoming more socially aware, and cries because they want your company.

This is a good time to start setting up some good sleeping habits with your baby. You don't have to keep it completely rigorous at this time. But having your own sleep schedule in place can make it much easier for you to get the baby to sleep when you want later on.

What Is Normal for Six to Nine Months?

A typical six to nine-month-old is going to sleep between fourteen to fifteen hours a day. This is split up between their naps and their nighttime sleep though, so don't be surprised if they sleep too much during the day and they aren't able to sleep at night. Many times, by this age, the baby is able to sleep for much longer stretches of time, which can mean some relief for the parents at night. Many of the babies in this age group are going to consolidate their naps down to about two, one in the morning and one in the afternoon.

This is also the period when most babies start sleeping through the night, though there will be some babies who don't yet. If your baby is able to sleep for about eight hours or a little more during the night, it means that they are learning how to settle back to sleep, and it is a great sign that you are raising a good sleeper.

Don't fret too much if your baby isn't sleeping straight for eight hours. Many babies are still waking up for some feedings during this stage. Many are ready for night weaning at this time if you choose to do it. Many times, when a baby wakes up during this time, it isn't because they are hungry. They may wake up for brief periods of time during the night. Some babies wake themselves up more and need help getting back to sleep. Others are able to fall right back to sleep without making a noise.

While major developmental milestones during this time could be partly to blame for the issues with sleeping during this time, another issue to watch out for is teething pain. If you suspect that the baby is waking up because of their teeth during this time, they may just need a little extra cuddling to help them get into a deep sleep.

Each child is going to be different. There are some babies who will be great sleepers with very little work from their parents. And then there are some babies who will need some extra time and patience from their parents to get into a good sleep schedule. And if you have big life events, illness, or traveling during this time, you will just need to roll with the changes and know that your baby may get off their sleep schedule for a bit. Maintaining a steady schedule can help get them back on track faster.

What Is Normal for Nine Months to One Year?

Most nine to twelve months old is going to sleep about fourteen hours a day, including two naps that are about one to two hours at a time based on your schedule. Some pediatricians do notice that babies this age will have different sleep patterns during this time. This could be because the baby is reaching some new milestones during this time or because they get more calories from solid foods, so they can sleep for longer.

If you haven't been able to get the baby to fall into a sleep pattern at this time yet, then now is the time to get started with it. These sleep training methods can do a great job at helping your baby get to sleep more easily, sleep for longer periods of time during the night, and can give you a break because they get on more regular hours. If you have trouble getting them on a schedule during this time, it is time to use some of the different sleep techniques we will discuss in this guidebook.

If your baby is able to sleep for about nine to ten hours at a time during the night, then it means the baby knows how to settle back into sleep when they wake up and it is a sign that you already have a good sleeper. At this time, it is time to do night weaning because most babies are not going to wake up as much at night due to hunger.

There are some babies who run into trouble with waking up at night and not falling asleep. These often show up with some major milestones in motor and cognitive development. And for some babies, it could be a sign of separation anxiety. You can go in and help calm them down a little bit, and usually, this is enough to get them back to sleep.

During this age, you need to stick with your consistent bedtime routine, keep the baby on a regular schedule as much as possible, and make sure the baby has plenty of chances to fall asleep all on their own.

What Is Normal for Toddlers?

If you do not work with your child at a young enough age, it is possible that they will suffer from sleep problems even when they reach older than one year of age. Knowing what to expect when your baby turns into the next stage of being a toddler can make it easier to come up with a sleep schedule that works well for them as well.

Most toddlers are going to be early risers. This is just how their system is set up so don't be upset if they come in to wake you up between six and seven in the morning. Whenever they wake up though is fine, as long as they get enough sleep and their rising time fits into the schedule that works for your family. If your child seems to be sleepy most of the morning, or they want a nap after only being up for a few hours, then they may need to go to bed earlier at night or be sent back to bed for another round of rest in the morning.

If your toddler wakes up around seven in the morning, you will want to aim for a nap around 9:30 in the morning. But as they grow, they will phase out of this nap time. Many one-year-olds to eighteen months old will start to phase out of this nap time, and that is fine. Just make sure that they have a little time for being quiet in the morning. Spend this time playing independently, listening to stories on CDs, or looking at books. They don't have to be completely asleep during this time, but the quiet time can help the child recharge for active periods during the day.

If your toddler needs it, or if they don't take that first-morning nap, then you will need to give them another round of rest after a good lunch. Most of the time, getting them to nap between 1:30 and 2 in the afternoon are the best. Make sure that the nap stays under two hours. If the child does end up napping too late in the afternoon, it may interfere with their ability to sleep at night. You can alter this nap schedule to fit your needs. Some kids may need to take a nap a little earlier, but make sure that they are getting this rest time in the afternoon.

The routine that you see from one home to another will vary; but generally, a toddler is going to fall asleep sometime between six and eight at night. This is plenty of time for the toddler to get their twelve hours of sleep at night and then they can still be up for a family breakfast and have time for the family at night. Try to schedule bath time for six at night and then give them some time to relax before a bedtime at seven. Or you can adjust this to work for your family. Just make sure that there is some winding down time before the baby has to head to bed.

Chapter 4:
Tools You Need for Success

No matter how hard you try, you can't make the baby sleep or do anything else for that matter. But while you can't force the baby to fall asleep, you do have some resources at your disposal that can help you encourage your baby to sleep. The baby has to be tired, or be ready for bed, but you can utilize some tools to help you to encourage the baby to reach that stage and get them out for some good shut-eye.

There are a variety of tools that you can use that will help your child to sleep. Some of them are going to be really effective, but others are going to really cause more problems than they are able to solve. You may find that your baby reacts better to some of these tools compared to others, and sometimes it takes a little bit of experimenting to get results. The tools that we are going to discuss in this chapter are going to help encourage sleep for your baby in ways that you aren't going to regret down the road.

These tools will safely and significantly encourage your baby to fall asleep, and can also help them stay asleep. Some of the criteria for tools to be listed in this guidebook include:

- It needs to elevate the degree of soothing that the baby gets helping to increase the odds that your baby will fall asleep and then stay asleep. While you can't make your baby fall asleep, you can certainly make it hard for them to stay awake.

- It functions for the whole time your child is sleeping. Anything that is on a timer will not count here because the timer can turn off the device.

- It can work without much parental involvement. For example, we are not going to recommend putting the baby in a car and driving them around. Sure, this gets most babies to fall asleep, but until self-driving cars come around, it includes a ton of parental involvement.

- The device is not you. Sure, you may be able to hold your baby and get them to sleep, but you are probably tired of doing that. None of these techniques are going to involve you as the parent getting the baby to sleep.

- It is something that you can wean the baby off of in the future in a gentle way. This means that you get the benefit of using the tool without worrying about whether you will have to fight to break them off it in the future.

Keep in mind that not all of the tools we are going to discuss will work for all ages. The ones that we choose are specific for babies to help you finally get that much-needed rest with them. Some will work until the baby is older, but don't be surprised if they kind of outgrow it.

A Note About You as The Sleeping Tool

One note here is to realize that we are not trying to make nursing, cuddling, or holding the baby to sleep a bad thing. And when you have a newborn, the only place you may be able to get them to sleep is on you. This actually gives you a lot of freedom and flexibility when they are first born to go out and meet friends and get out of the house.

With a newborn, cuddling the baby to sleep or nursing them to sleep may be the only thing that works for those high-need newborns. And that is not a bad thing. Nor are we spending time here saying that you should forgo the joys of having a little infant sleeping in your arms. If this is what you find the easiest when they are brand new, then go ahead and get the cuddles as much as you want.

What we are talking about here is a baby who has reached past the newborn stage and is much older, but who still fusses whenever they are put down. Doing this too much and for too long can lead to some troubles such as:

- Teaching the baby that sleeping with you or on you is the only way that they can fall asleep. This is not something that you can sustain over the long term.

- Making it hard to convince a baby who is older and who have spent their whole life sleeping on you that sleeping somewhere else is a good thing and this can be a challenge. This is how parents become stuck sleeping with a baby for many months.

- Creating a really unfeasible sleep or nap arrangement with older children.

- Unsafe sleep situations: An infant who is asleep on your lap on the couch when you are wide awake is not a big deal. But if you fall asleep with them there, it can be unsafe.

- The absence of any transition strategy to help get the baby to sleep independently.

So, while it is just fine to take that newborn and cuddle and hold them tight, but mindful that the goal here is to gradually foster safe, sustainable, and independent sleep. And for most families, this is the process of establishing sleep that doesn't always involve you.

White Noise

Now that we have looked at some of the basics that come with sleep for the baby, and the importance of not becoming a human mattress yourself, it is time to look at some of the best tools that can help your baby to fall asleep. The first option is known as white noise. This is often the most effective, easiest to implement and the least expensive sleep method for your baby.

There are some parents who don't want to invest in the machine or who feel that their baby will become addicted to this kind of noise. But this just puts them at a disadvantage because white noise is really so great for your baby and getting them to sleep. Plus, it is really easy to work with.

White noise can help reduce some of the stress that your baby may feel. What would a baby get stressed out about? Just about everything in this new and big world. They may be stressed because they are so tired, the world has a lot of stimulation, or because mom and dad are trying to put them to sleep without holding them. White noise can create a new safe space for the baby simply by blocking out all that extra stimulation.

White noise can actually help your baby to sleep. In fact, a good source of white noise is able to help the baby fall asleep easier and even keeps them asleep longer. This is because many babies have a sleep arousal period which happens between ever twenty to forty-five minutes. Some babies are not able to fall back to sleep after this arousal, so that means sleep time is over. White noise helps the baby to navigate around these arousals so they get some better sleep and it can block out any noise that keeps the baby awake.

Using a source of white noise can help your baby cry less. Most people throughout the world will use a type of shushing noise to help babies calm down. The white noise can help do this for you if you use it properly. The key is that the white noise needs to be louder than the crying.

In a recent study, it was suggested that babies who had a fan in their room were actually at a lower risk of SIDS compared to other babies. Nobody is quite sure why the fan seems to help. It could be due to the circulating air so the baby isn't rebreathing the same air that they exhaled. But it could do more with the noise that the fan makes. White noise, including that which comes from the fan, is able to reduce active sleep, which is the state of sleep where SIDS is the most likely to occur.

White noise can even help you as a parent fall asleep. If you happen to have your newborn sleeping in the same room as you, which is recommended for the first six months, you will find that they make a lot of noise that can keep you awake. They kick around, grunt, snort, fart, and make a lot of other noises. When you bring the white noise into your room, this can help to mask some of these small sounds so you are able to sleep better.

So, with all of these benefits, you may be curious about how you are going to use it to help your baby fall asleep. You can choose to purchase a white noise generator if you choose, but you don't have to. There are many white noise apps that are available on your tablet or phone. A clock radio that is set to static can do the trick as well. Sometimes using an air purifier or humidifier will make enough noise to do this.

When you have the device you want to use, turn the volume up so it is around 50 decibels, or about the level of someone taking a shower if you are standing in the bathroom with them. This shouldn't be uncomfortably loud. If you notice that it is bothering you a bit, then it is too loud. Leave this white noise in the same area where the baby will sleep and make sure that it is not going to turn off. Only use the white noise when the baby is asleep. When they are awake, you want to expose your baby to things like life, music, and speech.

Due to a rat study that was done in 2003, many people are worried about using a white noise machine to help their babies fall asleep. Researchers from the University of California published a study at this time where baby rats were raised in a sound deprivation chamber. In this chamber, they were exposed to loud and unceasing white noise the whole time they were "children." These baby rats then grew up to be kind of weird.

Because of this study, many parents are worried that using white noise is going to ruin their children. However, moderate use of the white noise, just when the baby is sleeping, is just fine and there is no evidence to suggest otherwise. If you are still concerned, you can always talk with your pediatrician to help you feel more comfortable before using this tool.

Swaddling

The next tool that you may want to consider using is swaddling. This is actually one of the oldest soothing techniques that have been used for thousands of years. It is actually shown to help babies sleep better. There are many reasons to consider swaddling your baby.

The first benefit is that swaddling can help your baby to cry less. In fact, one study found that swaddling reduced the crying rate by 28 percent. This is especially true during the first two months of the baby's life when they are more difficult to soothe.

Swaddling can also help your baby sleep longer and better. Swaddling will prevent the newborn from startling themselves awake with random arm movements when they are asleep. Newborns are sometimes able to wake themselves up accidentally by hitting themselves in the face. Swaddling can help reduce this risk.

Swaddling can help reduce the incidence of SIDS in some cases. Some of the evidence that shows how swaddling can reduce the SIDS risks in your baby include:

- Some studies show that there is a decreased amount of SIDS associated with babies sleeping swaddled on their backs.

- Parents who choose to swaddle their babies are more likely to lay that baby down on their backs.

- Although these babies sleep better, they are more arousable when exposed to noise.

- A retrospective eight-year study that looked at SIDS and infants who were swaddled found that there were no significant risks when the baby was swaddled and left on their backs.

- Sleeping while swaddled is able to hinder the ability of the baby to flip over on their stomach, a position that has been associated with SIDS.

- Swaddling can make it hard for a newborn to accidentally cover their face or their heads with the bedding.

Baby swaddling is almost like a lesson in origami. There are many different ways to do it and often the right way is whichever method you would prefer. You have been successful with swaddling your baby when the arms don't pop out when you are done.

Swaddling the baby with their arms right down at the side is often the most efficient because it is much harder for the baby to break out when their arms are straight. However, there are some babies who prefer to have their arms bent in the swaddle so you may need to experiment with it a bit. Either way, the successful swaddling technique is when the blanket is snug enough that the baby isn't able to wiggle about a lot but still loose enough that you can get two fingers in there.

The focus of swaddling should be on the upper body. The benefits come from keeping the arms as immobile as possible and close to the body. There aren't really any benefits to swaddling the lower body and doing it too tightly could result in hip dysplasia in the body.

Remember that no matter how good you get at swaddling; your little wiggly baby may be able to get out of it. If you find that your baby is just too good at getting out no matter how hard you work, there are some swaddle blankets out there that come with Velcro, which can make the process easier, especially when you are in the dark.

In addition, some babies are going to cry or fuss when they are being swaddled. This is a negative response to the whole process of being swaddled. This doesn't mean that the baby doesn't like swaddling or that they won't sleep better when they are swaddled. Don't let all that complaining fool you because they may really like it, they may have gotten used to what you are doing there and don't want to go to sleep.

Before you decide to start swaddling your baby, there are a few safety concerns you need to pay attention to include:

- Never lay the baby down on their stomachs when they are swaddled. Sleeping face down can increase the risk of SIDS by twelve times when the baby is swaddled. Always lay them on their backs.

- Let other people know the safety rules about swaddling if they are going to do it.

- When your baby has mastered the skill of flipping onto their stomachs, then you should stop swaddling altogether.

- Don't let the baby overheat. No matter what you are doing, swaddling or not, or what time of year, you want to make sure that you are not letting the baby get overheated.

Swaddling can be very comforting to many babies and this is a practice that has been done throughout the world for many generations. It can be a great way to make your baby comfortable and to get them to fall asleep much easier for you.

Using A Pacifier

A pacifier is a tool that a lot of people shy away from because they fear the baby will become addicted to it and it will be impossible to get rid of the habit. It can be hard, in the beginning, to get the baby to take the pacifier and you may have to try out a bunch of them in order to get the baby to take one. Then there are always issues with wondering whether the pacifier is going to hinder your efforts to nurse, although most of these myths have been debunked.

And after some time, you have to figure out how to get the baby to give up the pacifier.

However, it is worth it in many cases. Babies have a natural urge to suck on something, especially when they are sleeping, and the pacifier can help with this. Some of the reasons that you may want to consider using a pacifier for your baby include:

- Sucking on the pacifier while they fall asleep has been able to reduce the risk of SIDS.

- Pacifiers are very soothing for the baby. And when they are combined with some of the other soothing techniques, such as white noise and swaddling, they can help improve how well the baby sleeps and can reduce how often they cry.

- Introducing the pacifier after you finish breastfeeding can help meet the need of the baby to suck, while you get a break.

Babies may struggle against things that are essential or helpful for putting them to sleep. Some babies will show a lot of interest in a pacifier, and others won't care about it at all. This can raise a bit of a challenge when it comes to getting the baby to take a pacifier and use it to get them to sleep. But now that we know some of the benefits of using the pacifier, it may be something that you want to experiment with. Some of the things that you should try to get the baby to like their pacifier (if they do end up struggling) include:

- Buy a few different types of pacifiers. Each baby is going to take a different type, and even if one type worked for an older child doesn't mean that it will work for this child. Purchase a few different ones and save the ones that aren't used for later.

- Offer the pacifier at a time when the baby is not hungry. When a baby is starving, they are going to get angry when something that doesn't contain food is put in their mouth.

- Offer the pacifier at a variety of times during the day. Or try it on a different day.

- Experiment with the pull-out technique. This is when you place the pacifier into the mouth of the baby and then flick it a bit like you want to pop it out. The response of the baby is to naturally suck harder. This can help the baby get used to the pacifier and can get them to enjoy it.

- Try adding a little formula or milk to the tip to get them to take it.

Keep in mind that there are some babies who just won't take the pacifier. They may need to have another method to help them soothe at the end of the day. If your baby doesn't enjoy the pacifier, don't try to force it too much.

Baby Swings

Another method that you may try out is a baby swing. Your baby has been swinging sleeping since they were conceived. This swing, which is in the womb, is always rocking the baby around when you are up and moving during the pregnancy, so this is a natural movement that they are used to. This is why it shouldn't come as a surprise that your baby likes to swing and will fall asleep better when swinging. They like the movement which is why they fall asleep in the swing, in a rocking chair, and in the car. You can use this love of motion to help you get your baby to sleep.

Baby swings are a fantastic option because they provide you with three key elements when you are trying to get the baby to sleep. First, there is a consistent rocking motion that is similar to what the baby finds when they are in the womb providing the soothing that the baby is used to and sees as a natural condition for sleep.

Second, even when these swings are fully reclined, they will still make sure the baby is slightly upright. Many babies have a valve at the top of their stomach which is undeveloped still. This means that in some cases, their food, such as the formula or milk, will be pushed up. Sleeping inclined a little bit can help keep food inside the stomach. And unlike the popular crib wedges, which can be dangerous and can cause SIDS, these swings have some baby straps that will keep your baby in place.

And the number one benefit of using these crib swings is that they will help the baby learn how to gradually fall asleep all on their own.

One thing to note here is that the AAP or the American Academy of Pediatrics position on SIDS recommends against babies sleeping anywhere except on their back in an unadorned modern crib. They are against things like swings, pack and plays, bassinets, and any form of co-sleeping. Your overall goal should be for your baby to sleep as much as possible in a crib because this is considered the safest sleep area possible.

That does not mean you can't use the swing to help you out. Many parents will place the baby in the swing so they can fall asleep, being there and watching the whole time. Then, after the baby has had time to fall asleep and self-soothe for a bit, they will move the baby over to a crib and leave them in the safe sleeping arrangement, perhaps with some white noise to help.

However, there are some parents who find that their baby just won't fall asleep in the crib no matter what. They may try the white noise, the rocking, the swing, and everything else. But as soon as they lay the baby down, that baby is awake and crying again. If you are running into troubles getting the baby to sleep, discuss whether a baby swing is good for your baby with your pediatrician.

Most parents will choose to experiment with this baby swing at naptime. This makes it easier for you to watch how things go since you will be awake during this time. You can keep an eye out on the baby. This works for many parents who find that their baby sleeps just fine at night but struggles to stay asleep during the day for nap time.

Some of the steps that you can take to ensure your baby falls asleep when using the swing include the following:

- Put the swing in the area where your baby tends to sleep the most often. This could be in your room or somewhere near their crib.

- Use the right kind of white noise. This helps the baby fall asleep and can mask any of the noises that come from the swing.

- Set up the baby monitor so that you can hear what is going on with the swing.

- Never put the baby into the swing without having all the straps on.

- Begin by putting the swing on the highest speed that you are comfortable with. Once the baby is comfortable and is able to routinely sleep in the swing, you can then go through and experiment a bit with the speed.

- Consider swaddling. Most babies who use a swing are going to be swaddled, but this is not a requirement.

- To start, see if the baby is able to fall asleep all on their own in the swing. If this works, then you win! If it doesn't work (and it won't for all babies), you may need to use a few other techniques to help you out.

If the baby struggles, you can try a few of these options:

- Put something that smells the same as a mom in the swing next to them. This can be a toy or even the shirt that mom wore all day.

- Consider nursing and feeding the baby and rocking them fully to sleep. Then put them into the swing and let them sleep there.

All of these methods can be great tools to ensure that your baby is going to fall asleep at night. Some parents find that they need to use a combination of these techniques to get their baby to sleep. The trick here is to mess around until you find a method that works for you and that will help your baby fall asleep.

Chapter 5:
Develop a Sleep Schedule

Now it is time to talk about setting up a sleep schedule for your baby. This is another tool that you can use which is foundational to how effective all the tools we discussed in the other chapter will be. If you ever try to put your baby to sleep when they are too tired or not tired enough, you are going to end up with a lot of hassle when you try to get the baby to sleep. Most of the tools that we have talked on are about how to get your baby to finally fall asleep. But now we are going to talk more about when to get the baby to go to bed.

Even if a baby is tired, they are not going to just nod off when they need to sleep. In fact, most will stay awake far past when they need to fall asleep, and they will easily get fussy and angry the longer they go. When they are awake for too long, many babies are going to get crabby and can be difficult to soothe. Even worse, if you let the baby stay up too long, it can impact their sleep hormones and their stress hormone production which can make it harder for them to sleep in the first place.

Then the problem can go the other way as well. If the baby hasn't been up long enough, then they aren't going to be tired enough to actually fall asleep. If their nap goes too late in the afternoon, for example, and then you try to put them to bed too early, they may get mad when you try to put them down and they aren't tired.

This is why having a sleep schedule, or at least as close to a schedule as you can, can ensure that your baby will get enough sleep, but won't fight because you are putting them down too often. But this brings up the question on how I will know when it is time to get the baby to sleep. If you are lucky, the baby will tell you. You just need to pay attention to what they are telling you to catch it.

Signs That Your Baby Is Tired
Some babies are going to seem really happy, no matter how long they have been awake. Some will seem fine, and then all of a sudden, they will have a major breakdown out of nowhere. Other babies are going to show you some great signals when they are feeling tired and you can catch them before a meltdown starts to happen. Each baby is different and you need to learn what signals they will send off. Some of the signals that the baby is likely to show off when they start to feel tired includes:

- Yawning.

- Blinks that are done in slow motion.

- Rubbing their eyes.

- Seems like they are interested in eating, but they won't eat anything when the food is offered to them.

- They make movements that are more jerky than usual.

- They stop making eye contact with you.

- They start to lose interest in activities or toys.

- They cry for a new reason at all.
- They start to get fussy.

Tired toddlers and preschoolers are often going to take this to another level. They are more likely to have some tantrums and can get physical, such as throwing and grabbing things or even hitting. Even older children and teenagers can have some signs of being tired, even though they are less likely to show these outward signs of being overtired.

The hardest part about some of these sleepy signs is that most babies are really unreliable about giving them. Or, which happens more often than not, by the time the baby starts to exhibit these signs of being tired, they have reached the point of being overtired. This is why it is so important to keep one eye on how your child is behaving, and the other eye on the clock. If you have gotten them on a good sleeping schedule, you will be able to predict when the child will start to be tired and can take the right precautions to get them to bed before things start to explode.

How long your child is able to stay awake comfortably can depend on a variety of factors, including their age and temperament. And then there are days when, even though you have figured out a sleeping schedule with them, it seems like they are able to throw themselves out of it and nothing will appease them. This is perfectly normal and in fact, it is something that you should just prepare for at some point. If there are ever some big life changes, a change in the schedule, or if you travel with your children, then this can throw off their sleep schedule for that time period as well.

This is a big experiment to find out what works for your child. What works for a nap schedule in one family may not work that well for your family. And you may find that each child is going to react to their sleep schedule in a different manner. Some kids may be more of night owls and like having later naps so they can stay up later, and others may like to get up earlier and get to bed at a decent time so they can do it.

Of course, remember that the timing of naps can make a big difference as well. If you put the baby down for an early nap, and then expect them to stay up until late without any other naps, then you are going to end up with a very grumpy baby. However, if you put the baby down for a late nap and then expect them to go to bed at an early hour, you are going to have a baby who is not happy that you are trying to put them to bed early. You need to make sure that there are at least a few hours, but not too many hours, between the last nap and bedtime to make it easier to get your baby to sleep.

It is fine to take your child's lead here. Just make sure that they are getting the recommended number of hours of sleep so that they don't get overly tired and they can grow and develop properly. Over time, you will be able to get the child on a steady schedule with their own circadian rhythm, and bedtime won't be as big of a hassle.

Chapter 6:
Sleep with Assistance Plan (SWAP)

Now, we have spent some time looking at some of the best sleep assistance plans to get that baby to sleep. Sometimes, just using a few of the tools that we discussed before won't be enough to get that baby to sleep. You may need to come up with a plan of attack to help get them comfy and into bed. The methods that we are going to talk about in this guidebook are going to be no cry methods.

While there are many people out there who are proponents of the cry it out methods, these are not always the best choice to go with. Studies have shown that the crying out method can be bad on the baby, causing anxiety and many other conditions. These crying it out methods can also be hard on the parents who have to listen to the crying and can't go in to help. Plus, for all that pain and suffering, the crying it out methods is often not that effective.

We are going to focus on easy no-cry methods that will help to get baby to sleep through the night, without any of the issues that can come with the crying it out method. And the first method we are going to take a look at is known as SWAP, or the sleep with assistance plan.

When Is the Best Time to Teach My Baby to Sleep?
While it may seem crazy, there is the easiest time to teach the baby to sleep. Remember that this is the easiest time, not that this is necessarily going to

be easy. The rule of thumb that we are going to follow here is the younger the better. This can help the baby develop the skills they need to get to bed at a decent time, to sleep through the night, and to grow and develop the way that they should in the future.

The easiest time for the parent to work on teaching babies to fall asleep all on their own is between the ages of two to four months. If you have a baby in this age range, you may think that this is crazy. For some babies, this process is never easy, so think of this time as the "less horrible time" to sleep train. The process doesn't really get easier when the baby gets older, so you may as well do it when they are younger.

Why is this age range a good one to help teach the baby how to sleep? The first reason is that the baby is young enough that you can still use the tools we already discussed in a safe and effective manner. And when you are trying to convince that four-month-old of yours who likes to fall asleep with nursing that it is time to go to sleep without nursing, these tools can be essential. Trying to remove nursing from sleep can be really hard for a baby and these power tools can help make it easier and they work the best on babies who are a bit younger.

The younger baby is still learning the basics of falling asleep which means they are more malleable especially when compared to older children. An 11-month old is firmly convinced by that time that there is only one way for them to fall asleep. Convincing them to change those habits can be almost impossible. But the two to four-month-old doesn't know which way there is to fall asleep, and you can be the one to train them.

There are also some fairly predictable sleep setbacks that can occur between four and nine months. These can include separation anxiety, teething, and several sleep regressions. When you start early, you are giving yourself a chance to establish some strong foundation for good sleep in the baby before they run into these potential issues.

Teaching the Baby to Sleep Using the Fundamentals

Teach your child to sleep on their own. This means that you need to introduce the right sleep associations and new techniques to help them get a better quality of sleep. This also means that you will be teaching them a new way to fall asleep compared to what they may have done in the past. We will look at several different techniques that you can use that fit under the category of sleeping with assistance and you can choose the one that you think will work the best with your little one or the one that works the best with your current family schedule. However, any effort to teach the baby to sleep should be based on a solid foundation that will include the following:

- Start out with a bedtime.

- If you don't already have one for your baby, then now is the time to set one. You can pick the bedtime that works the best at your home; just make sure to get one set up.

- Have a bedtime that is age-appropriate and consistent.

- There are lots of guidelines on when to get the child to sleep based on when you get up in the morning and what age the child is. Pick out that bedtime and stick with it, even on the weekends.

- Have a bedtime routine.

- It doesn't have to be a very long bedtime routine, just long enough to signal to the brain that it is time for that child to go to bed. Twenty to thirty minutes is usually long enough. You can give them a warm bath, brush their teeth, and read a few stories before sending them off.

- Keep the room dark.

- You want to make sure the room your baby is sleeping in can be kept dark. A lot of light can distract the baby and may even mess with their own circadian rhythms.

SWAPS to Help Your Baby Fall Asleep Without You

Now it is time to take a look at some of the sleeping plans that you can try with your baby. The SWAPs are nice because they will generally involve a more gradual approach to getting your baby to sleep, will require a lot of parental involvement, and can take a bit longer to implement. But even though they do take longer and need more involvement from you, they are very successful for most babies and you will be happy with spending this time. Let's take a look at the different approaches and what they all mean!

More Soothing

The first method we are going to look at is the more soothing method. This is a method that works well for babies who are under four months of age or ones who are older and have high-needs. It can also work for babies who have a lot of reflux that tends to keep them up.

As we discussed before, younger babies are going to need a lot more soothing to help them settle to sleep at night. Especially when it comes to a newborn, their default source of soothing will be you. They will fall asleep on your lap while you wear them during nursing, and everywhere else that they are close to you. While cuddling with your baby can be nice and we all enjoy doing it, we do need to have some time to take care of older children, work, or do other things without a baby attached. Having a baby who refuses to sleep for more than twenty minutes if they are not held by you can become a problem. The same can happen with children who are high-needs, or who have colic or reflux, and will need more soothing than others.

The solution for this is to provide more soothing. And the best way to do this is to use some of the tools that we discussed in previous chapters. People may choose to skip this step because they believe that independent sleep means that they shouldn't use any tools. Yes, you are trying to move forward and get to a place where the child is able to fall asleep on their own during bed and naps but the goal is not to go without any sleep tools. It's using the right sleep tools and to get them from having to fall asleep on you.

You can use any combination of the tools that we discussed in the other chapters. You may even need to spend some time rocking them to sleep while swaddled, or with a pacifier, and then leaving white noise on to help them fall asleep. While it does require some work from you for a bit, it is worth the time and can be a great way to teach your child to fall asleep. As they get more used to the process, you can work on reducing how long you personally comfort them until you can lay them down in the crib and they fall asleep on their own.

FIO or Fuss It Out

This method will work just fine for most babies who are older than two months of age. This will utilize all of the tools that we talked about, as long as they are age appropriate for your child. You will hold onto the baby, rocking them or letting them sleep on you until the baby is drowsy and calm. Then, while they are still a little bit awake, you will lay them in the crib and walk away.

If the baby is under three months, set a timer for ten minutes. If they are older, you may want to set the timer for a little bit longer. You may hear them grumble a bit and move around, but if you got them to a drowsy state and you have the white noise and other tools present, then you will find they can get themselves to sleep with a few minutes of fussing.

During this stage, you don't want to let them cry it out. If they reach this point, then the tool is not going to help and they will simply wake themselves up. This is why it's important to let the baby get nice and tired and almost asleep before you try it out.

If your baby does fall asleep with this method, this means that you are successful and should be able to continue to use this method with the baby falling asleep all on their own. But if you go through that ten minutes on the timer and the baby hasn't fallen asleep, you have a few decisions to make depending on what is happening and these include:

- The baby is calm, but still awake. If the baby is happy, just leave them alone and see what happens. They may start to get angry, they may fall asleep, or they may just play around for a bit before falling asleep.

- The baby is grumbly and a little fussy, but they are not screaming. The fussy is fine for now. They may just need to adjust a bit before they fall asleep. Wait a bit longer and see what happens.

- The baby starts to scream. You will want to go in and soothe the baby. If you can just walk in and give them their pacifier back or turn the white noise up a bit, and they calm down, then do that. Only pick them up if the crying continues and you can't get them to fall asleep.

While it is possible that your baby will start to cry with this method, it is not a traditional cry it out method. This is a decision to give the baby a brief amount of time to see what will happen if you give them a little space. While it isn't going to work for each baby, some will fall asleep fast if they get removed from the situation. And unlike the cry it out methods, the fuss it out method has a time limit and the parent will go back in. If the baby keeps crying and nothing works, the parents simply go back to their traditional method of sleeping and try something else another night.

The Double Take

This method is best for babies who are under four months old but sometimes kids of older ages will find this beneficial as well. For this one, you are going to soothe your child fully to sleep, picking out any method that works the best for you. When the baby is fully asleep, you can place them in their bed. Once you lay them down, you will wake them up just a little bit. You don't want to wake them up completely, just a little bit. Then allow the baby to fall back into a deep sleep, lying in their own bed.

Some parents have trouble with this one because they don't like the idea that they might undo all the hard work they did by waking the baby back up. But this technique can work because it helps the baby identify that they are in their own bed. Then, when they wake up later in the night at some point, they won't be surprised to be here. Also, make sure to remove any of the unsustainable sleep associations before you wake them up. This means take the pacifier out or make sure you stop the breastfeeding before letting them fall asleep.

You may wonder how awake the baby needs to be when you do this method. You want them to be a little more than eyes barely flutter open. You know that you have gotten the right amount of awake when the baby is grumbling about your behavior.

This is a great technique to work on but remember that it may not be the cure-all to all sleep association challenges. For some babies, it may work, but other times it may not. If you were successful with this double take method with your child for a few nights, and you don't see that there is a big improvement in how well your child sleeps, then this may not be the technique for them and you need to move on and try another one.

Gradual Weaning
This technique is a good one to use with babies who are between two to six months old. As the name suggests, this gradual weaning process is simply taking baby steps to slowly do less of whatever you currently do to help the baby fall asleep. There are a lot of different approaches that you can use to work with gradual weaning, but they all boil down to the ideas that are expressed in this haiku:

- Gradually do less

- Tears and complaints may ensue

- Press on regardless

Some parents may then wonder how they are going to be able to put the baby down awake without the pacifier, sleeping on the chest, nursing, or rocking. They may have spent a lot of time doing these things in the past for their baby and worry about what will happen when they stop.

There are a number of things that you can do here. If the baby is used to falling asleep with a pacifier, consider stopping the use during the day first. Then take it away during short naps, and slowly take it away as they start to fall asleep at night. If the baby likes to be rocked to sleep, you can start by rocking them for shorter amounts of time before putting them in their crib and letting them self-soothe. You can even consider laying them down with some white noise and then rocking the crib a little.

The method that you choose is going to vary depending on what your baby likes to do to fall asleep. Here are examples of how you would do the gradual weaning process if your baby is one who likes to cuddle before they can go to sleep on their own at night

The baby is used to falling asleep while they are snuggled in tight next to you. So, the first step would be to put a small space, about an inch or two, between you and the baby. They may not be too happy about this, and they will try to shift over each time that you move. You may need to use your hand to gently weigh them down and maintain some space. The baby will fuss a bit and the bedtime routine may take a bit longer, but eventually, it will work.

Over time, you decide to expand the distance between you and the baby to maybe six inches. The baby is really not happy about this and tries to move closer. But you are firm and loving at this time. You hold your hand gently on their stomach while singing quietly to them. And after a little bit, she falls asleep.

The next move is when you will put a one-foot gap between you and the baby, and it takes even less time to fall asleep. However, the baby still wakes up frequently at night and you have to spend a lot of time singing with the hand on their belly.

This next step is when the gap between you and your baby is as long as your arm. You still keep your hand on the belly during this time, but you sing or use words, but you end this after three minutes, before pretending to be asleep. Keep pretending to be asleep, even if the baby is fussing or playing around. It will work to get them to sleep.

You are working to create space at bedtime, but now you need to remove your hand from your stomach. The baby may try to move over to you, but you simply must put them back in their spots. You continue to use some words or sing, and within a few minutes, the baby falls asleep.

After this time, you will then want to move the baby to the bed. The baby will probably fuss when you first try to get them to sleep in the bed without any holding. You may need to put your hand on their belly again and sing and talk for some time to get them to sleep.

This can take some time for you to get them used to, but with less and less contact over time, you will be able to get the baby used to sleep on their own, and they will be able to fall asleep simply by being put in their bed at night.

Evaluating How the SWAP Is Going

Sometimes the plan is not going to go as smoothly as you would like and you may be convinced that you are now doomed. But as with any type of experiment that you do, some things are going to work and some things just won't work for you. Some days you will find that things go more smoothly for you than others. If you feel like SWAP is the best fit for you, then you need to commit to it for at least five to seven days before seeing results. Mastering a new skill is going to take time and some commitment, but if you stick with it, you are going to see the results. Some of the signs that you are on the right track and that this is the right plan for you include:

- *You find that bedtime is now a more enjoyable activity that all participants will enjoy.*

- *Your child is able to sleep for a longer period of time with fewer interruptions.*

- *Your child will stay asleep in the exact location that you put them in all night long.*

- *You are starting to feel confident enough to work on these strategies even during naps. Or, if you have already done them to work on naps, you find that the naptime is getting longer or your child is able to fall asleep much easier at nap.*

- *You are already moving towards a solid age appropriate night sleep and feeding schedule.*

However, these plans are not always going to work for every family. If you committed yourself consistently to SWAP for a week or more, and some of the things below are not true for you, it may be time to re-evaluate your plan and figure out if you are doing it right, or if you need to try out a different method to get your results. Some of the reasons that your plan may not be working for you include:

- It is not the right strategy for your baby. Each baby is different and one of the strategies above may not be right.

- You are not being consistent. You have to be consistent all of the time, or you are not going to see the results that you want.

- You got stalled. You may have started out with all of the best intentions to change up things during bedtime, but then you got scared. Instead of continuing, you made some smaller changes and then stop. You don't want to hang out around here if you want to see some results with getting your baby to sleep.

- A growth spurt, regression, illness, or travel came up and you weren't able to get the results. This happens, but you just need to reset the clock and start again. Try to pick out a time to try these techniques when none of the above is going on.

When you have put in your best efforts to implement a SWAP and it is a huge mess, then this is not a good plan for you and it is time to stop. While these are great plans that can help you get your baby to sleep, some babies are not going to respond well to them. And no matter how good a plan may be, if your baby doesn't respond to them, then they are not the right one for you. Sometimes it's just because the plan is not the right one for the baby, and sometimes it is because the baby is too young. If your child is between the ages of two months to four months, it may be time to push the pause button and come back to try it out later. Or, the problem is that SWAP is not the right option for you. That's okay, we have plenty of other methods that you can try out to help your baby sleep through the night.

Chapter 7:
Sleep Learning Independence Plan (SLIP)

In the last chapter, we focused a lot on working with gradual strategies that could help your baby become an independent sleeper. These strategies are often effective for most parents and they are usually a good place to start. However, there are some circumstances where these strategies aren't going to work that well for you and for your baby. Some of the reasons that these SWAP strategies may not work well include:

- Sleep is so bad for the baby that slowly working on it for a few weeks is not a good option.

- Your emotional and physical reserves are on empty. The SWAP strategies can be great, but you do need to have some energy in reserves to work on them.

- You have already tried doing some of the SWAP methods and they aren't successful for you.

Another option that you may want to try out is to sleep train without parental assistance. This can be known by a few different names including the CIO, cry it out, or Ferberizing. Fundamentally, they are all going to come down to placing the baby into a space that is safe for them when it is time to go to sleep, and then letting them figure out how to fall asleep on their own. This is going to involve quite a few tears and many parents are not fond of the cry it out methods.

There are a lot of people who are against the crying it out methods. They think that all that crying can be hard on the baby, that it can make the baby feel abandoned, and that it will result in long-term issues for the baby. Plus, some parents find that they have trouble listening to the crying for very long; and some kids can keep that crying up for a very long time.

Whether or not you decide to use a cry it out a plan with your child, it is going to depend on various factors. If the temperament of your child is right for this one, you may only have to do it a few times and the baby will go to sleep. If you have tried out some of the other methods and they didn't work, then this might be something to try. And you need to make sure that your own nerves are able to handle it as well. There are also some babies who can seemingly cry for hours on end. These cry it out methods is probably not the best option for them.

Should I SLIP or Not?
The next question that you may have about this sleep learning independence plan is whether or not to use them. The whole point of working with this plan is to teach the baby how to sleep on their own, without the help of the parent, because the involvement of the parent isn't working anymore and it may even be hindering how well the baby can establish their own healthy sleep schedule. SLIP is more of a mindful parenting strategy that is used to help older babies to sleep on their own without having the parent nearby. They can generally involve some tears or complaints during the process, and these techniques work well for families who have not had much success with using the SWAP techniques that we talked about before or for whom severe sleep deprivation is causing issues right now.

At this point, you may be curious as to whether SLIP is the right technique for your family. Here is a checklist that you can go through to help you reach the conclusion on whether to use this or not. If you are able to answer yes to most of these questions, then it is probably time to start using SLIP.

Is the Baby At Least Six Months Old?

For younger babies, you can use some of the sleeping tools that we talked about before. SLIP generally works better with older children but take into account the temperament of your child to determine if these will work for them as well.

The Baby Has Chronic Issues with Sleep Deprivation.

IF your baby is getting quite a bit less sleep than they should, or they wake up a bunch of times during the night, then the baby is probably sleep deprived.

The Issue Here Is the Lack of Independent Sleep.

The SLIP technique is to help ingrain independent sleep in the baby. It can sometimes be applied to night weaning or even to early waking but it is going to work to deal with the baby's inability to fall asleep on their own.

Everything Else Hasn't Worked.

SLIP is often used as a last resort because it isn't as gentle on the baby as the other methods.

The Baby Isn't Suffering from Some Medical Complications.

Reflux, fevers, and colds can really make it hard to get the baby to sleep on their own. Consider waiting until after the issue is fixed before starting.

Baby Is in A Safe Space.
Make sure that the baby is left in a safe place when implementing SLIP. This can include their crib.

Both You and Your Partner Agree to Do This.
This is going to be a tough few days, so there isn't time for the two of you to fight over it. If you are still fighting with your partner about sleep, then don't get started with SLIP.

You Are Able to Maintain A Schedule That Is Consistent During That Time.
Sleep training is not something that you try to do the weekend before a big holiday. Find at least a few weeks when you can stick with a consistent schedule.

You Have A Good Night Vision Monitor.
If you don't have this, it doesn't mean that you can't work with SLIP, but it does help. It can help you to tell if the baby is asleep without walking into their room and risking them waking up on you.

You Are Committed.
You must be fully committed here. Your baby is going to try and get you to come back in and hold them and get them to sleep. If you do this, then you

are going to send a mixed message and you will never get them to do this sleep technique.

How to Implement SLIP at Night
As with the SWAP technique that we talked about in the previous chapter, SLIP is going to work best if you try it at night because the child will already be biologically set up to go to sleep at night. There are a few things that need to happen in order to make the SLIP technique work for you.

The first step is to make sure that you get the baby down for naps using any means necessary. You do not want the child to be overly tired when it is time to go to bed at night. It doesn't matter which method you use at this point: the car, a stroller, or rocking with you. For the next few days, make sure that you get those naps. You can work on independent sleeping at naptime later. Let's just focus on getting them to sleep independently at night for now. With that said, avoid those catnaps. These are cheating naps and won't give your baby the quality rest they need.

You can keep up with that consistent bedtime routine. This is a good way to help soothe the baby into sleep without having to do all of the work or all the nursing and cuddling. If you do nurse them before bed, which is fine, you just need to change up the order sometimes. For example, if your bedtime routine was a bath, books, boob, and then the bed, you would have to change it to boob, bath, books, and bed so that the baby doesn't get used to falling asleep while eating.

If the baby is swaddled during this time, it is fine to keep up with it, as long as you know they can't or they won't flip over. If you feel that the baby could potentially flip over at some time, then you should avoid swaddling while you are sleep training. If your child uses a pacifier and sleeps all night with it, this can eventually cause some sleep association problems that you will have to work on.

Before you get started with this method, make sure that the sleep location you choose for the baby is as safe as possible. Setting them down in their own crib is the best option, but also check out for other hazards. Are there any dangling cords the baby can reach? Can the baby climb out of the crib or fall out? Is the crib clear of any hazards like pillows, bumpers, blankets, or stuffed animals? Does the crib or any other furniture present a tip over hazard that you need to work with?

Make sure that from here, the baby is put down to sleep at the right bedtime. This should be the time that the child was historically falling asleep in the past. The key word here is sleep. If you spent an hour rocking the baby to sleep every night before they went out, then the bedtime would not be at the time when you began the rocking. It would be when the baby was asleep. This is going to be your new bedtime so get comfortable.

If you say anything to the baby before you leave the room, or before bedtime, then you need to be consistent with it here. Your baby is going to be very receptive to language and they will understand what you are saying, even if they aren't able to speak it themselves. Say something positive that helps explain what is going on without making the baby feel worried. Be firm, loving, and consistent in this.

After the bedtime routine is done and the room is safe and comfy, lay the baby down in their own bed before leaving the room. There are some strategies here that will have you camp out in the room because having your presence there can be helpful in the soothing process. However, many parents find that the opposite is true and them being in the room can make the baby more upset because they want to be picked up and cuddled. It can also create an issue with object permanence where the baby will come to expect that you will sit there in the room when they wake up at night, and when you aren't there, it can cause some issues.

If one of the parents is going to have more trouble with this process than the other, then it may be time to send one of them away. Letting them sit in the hallway or near the door and hear the crying, and feel guilty at the same time, can be detrimental to how well this process would go. That parent is the one who will give in and all the hard work will be lost. Sometimes this is the mom and other times it can be a dad. Whoever it may be, consider sending them outside or to another part of the house so the crying doesn't bother them as much.

After you lay the baby down for the night, give them some time to figure out how they are going to fall asleep without you. The baby may be sad, furious, angry, or even a combination of things. Ask yourself some questions here. Is the baby safe, fed, and loved? If you can answer yes to these, then you have done your job. From here, the baby is working on something that is new and it frustrates them. While it can be hard to listen to, it is fine for the baby to feel frustrated sometimes.

With this method, don't give up! Have faith that your child is going to be able to figure this out and that they will learn how to sleep without you. No, the baby is not going to want to, and they won't make it easy. But your baby has the ability to do this just fine. Going in now is just going to sabotage your goal of improving sleep and if you give in, it guarantees that the next time is worse. Just keep strong and it will get better.

Should I Check in or Not?

SLIP is based on the idea that your child must learn how to sleep without any unsustainable sleep associations. Typically, if you are the one who provides that sleep association in the form of cuddling, feeding, nursing, or rocking, then it is not going to be good if you go and check in on the baby. If they are still awake, the baby will expect that you are going to provide them with the sleep association that they are looking for.

When you fail to provide this, which you should fail to do this if you are fully committed to not going back to your old way of doing things, the baby is not going to be happy and they will be furious. They are used to doing things a certain way and you are not going along with the plan which can make the baby very unhappy.

For most babies, if you go back into the room to check on them, this is going to make things more difficult. This is why the full extinction method is the best one if you want to make SLIP work. For this one, you will place the child down while they are fully awake, making sure they are comfortable and safe, and then you don't return until after they are asleep.

There are also other SLIP methods that go against this plan. For example, Dr. Ferber suggested a method that is more of a graduated extinction. This method has the parent go back in for some brief checks at progressively longer intervals. You would start going in after three minutes, then after five more minutes, and then after ten minutes. With this approach, your child will probably cry horribly throughout each visit. Regardless, you will go in to make sure they are safe and then remind them that it is time for them to go to sleep before leaving the room again.

There is evidence that shows how both the graduated and the full extinction method are effective when it comes to improving sleep outcomes. But there isn't any evidence that shows how one is better than the other. Most parents seem to enjoy graduated extinction more because they feel that checking in periodically is more loving to the baby. There isn't really evidence to support that this is the better method, but if it makes you feel better while using the cry it out method, then go for it.

If you do decide to make a brief visit into your child during these methods, the five-minute plan may be the best one to try out. There is not really an ideal schedule when it comes to checking in on the baby during SLIP, but there are some key elements that should be present to make the graduated extinction plan work for you:

- It is simple so there are no user errors.

- Each interval ends up being longer than the previous ones.

- These intervals need to be long enough so that your child has a chance to fall asleep on their own.

Any schedule of visits that can meet these criteria will work just fine. Make it work for your needs. With the five-minute plan, you go in at five minutes, then go in ten minutes after the first visit, and then fifteen minutes after the second visit and on down the line until the baby falls asleep. When you go into the room, you do not pick up the child but spend time reiterating the soothing words that were used during bedtime. And make sure that you leave the room before the baby falls asleep.

Watch Out for The Extinction Burst

For most babies, the SLIP method is going to have a few nights that are challenging for the parents and then there is a dramatic and immediate improvement in how they sleep. There are other babies who will continue to cry longer and louder. You may find that you are not so confident in SLIP and how it can work for your baby. Or maybe you were successful with SLIP and then after a few weeks you find that your happy baby is up and crying again. If the latter has happened to you, then you are going through what is known as the extinction burst.

SLIP is often known as an extinction therapy that has the parent work to make any undesirable behavior, in this case, sleep, become extinct because you no longer reinforce or reward the behavior. And for about seventy percent of the parents who try it, this method is effective. They will spend a few days up to a week working on getting their baby to sleep at night and listening to the baby cry during that time. But once the week is over, the baby will be able to get put into bed and fall asleep without all the fighting and crying any longer.

However, for the remaining parents, the baby is going to start aping up on how much they cry. Or they may take a break for a few days from the crying and then they resume the crying again. This resumption is going to be known as an extinction burst where the child is doing even more of the behavior that you are trying to extinguish now that you took the reinforcer away. What can you do about this? Nothing really. You just have to stick with the plan and ride it all out until it is done.

The only thing that you can do here is to wait it out and hope that it ends before you lose your mind. And this is probably why these SLIP methods have just a bad reputation in the long term. They may work for some parents but others just can't deal with the weeks of going through all the crying. Sure, it will get better, but it can be hard on the nerves even if it doesn't require a lot of involvement from the parent.

This is why you need to carefully choose the sleep method that you want to use in your family. Many people go with the SWAP methods because, yes, they do need to be involved, but at least it doesn't require hours of crying to get the baby to sleep. SLIP can work well for a lot of parents and after a few days, the crying will be done and you will have a baby who can fall asleep on their own. But, if the baby doesn't fall asleep, and keeps going on with this trend, it can make for some very long nights.

Picking which of these sleep methods you want to go with can sometimes be a challenge. They both have pretty high success rates, and they can both works based on your baby and what they are like. You may have to experiment with a few different options to see which one is the best for you and for your baby. And you must remember that no matter how good the method may be, it is never going to work overnight.

Heidi Oster

Chapter 8:
If Night Waking Starts to Happen Again?

If you have gotten to this part of the guidebook, then congratulations! You have successfully used either SLIP or SWAP to help foster some independent sleep patterns in your baby, at least during bedtime. Some parents may have even gone so far as to move these techniques over to nap time as well. You have taught your child a very important life skill!

Chances are after you are successful with these techniques; you are going to see a dramatic and immediate reduction in the number of times the baby is up and moving during the night, especially if you used some of the sleeping tools that we discussed before. This is a big win for you as a parent so go ahead and celebrate a little bit.

This, however, isn't the end of the story. SLIP and SWAP are all about being able to fall asleep independently without any unsustainable sleep associations. However, they are not always a free pass to getting the baby to completely sleep through the night. You have created a possibility for the child to sleep through the night, but there are still going to be some night waking during this time.

It is not time to come up with a plan to address these extra awake times at night. And the plan that you come up with is going to be very dependent on the reason that your child is waking up in the first place. There are usually two main reasons why your baby is still waking up at night even after using SLIP and SWAP. These reasons include:

- They are hungry and need food.

- They lost their sleep association such as a pacifier, cuddling, or rocking.

- Let's take a look at each of these and explore what you can do to try and eliminate the baby waking up so many times during the night.

Waking and Eating

If your baby was routinely eating during the night before sleep training, then they are going to either expect or need to do this even after you have established the independent sleep. If you did this sleep training with a younger baby, they may not have reached the right developmental stage to go all night without needing food. If you did this with an older baby, they may be capable of going a long time without eating but they are used to these night feedings and it may take some time to shift their calories all over to the daylight hours.

For a child who is nursing, it is sometimes hard to know how much food they have taken in. Some are able to guzzle a ton of milk in just a few minutes; some will take a few minutes just to get things going. And some will get more than others. It isn't always an easy formula to get how much they eat from how long they nurse because this will vary for each baby.

Sometimes it is easier when the baby will take a bottle simply because you know exactly how much they are consuming at all points of the day. Maybe your baby is only drinking a few ounces for each feeding but then they demand many bottles throughout the night. Or maybe the baby is able to guzzle down a few large bottles. If you know how much they are taking in, you can consider the total volume consumed at night as a percentage of daily intake.

Let's say that your six-month-old takes in about 28 ounces of formula a day and then wake up four times at night to drink two ounces each time. Even though the individual feedings are pretty small, over the total of the night, she is taking in eight ounces, or about 30 percent of her intake.

Regardless of the age of your baby, if they are eating often or they camp on the boob all night, you can and should assume that they are consuming a substantial amount of food. And if you still aren't sure if your baby is eating a lot during the night, some of the other signs you can look for include:

- Having to change the diaper a few times at night to avoid big leaks.

- The morning diaper is so full that it is falling off and can't hold anymore.

- The baby isn't starving for food when they first wake up in the morning.

If you are doing sleep training with a younger baby, you will just need to feed them during these times. They are used to getting those calories at night and will just wake up more if you don't provide them to the baby. Just make sure that you don't let the baby fall asleep while holding onto the bottle or nursing. This will just bring out that sleep association again and can make things difficult down the road. Feed the baby until they are full and then when they are still a little bit awake, you can lay them back down in the crib and leave.

If your baby is a little bit older, it may be time to start minimizing their intake and their meals during the night and moving these feedings to other times. Make sure that the baby is well fed (don't overdo it or they may have an upset stomach) but make sure that they have enough they won't be hungry a few hours later. As they start to move to solids and more substantial foods, the baby should be able to go most, if not all, of the night without needing to eat. If they still act like they need a lot of food during this time, it may just be the fact that they have sleep association with the bottle or the breast, and you need to work on breaking that habit.

Baby Wakes Up but Is Not Hungry

There are sometimes other reasons that the baby will wake up at night besides being hungry. The first reason may be that the baby hasn't quite mastered the art of going back into their deep sleep mode without your assistance. While you have done a great job of taking those first steps to remove yourself from bedtime, there is a chance that your baby is going to keep waking up periodically for the first few nights, and maybe even longer, expecting you to go back to those behaviors they are used to.

Being able to establish these independent sleep patterns means that you need to be steadfast and not do whatever habit you did before using SLIP or SWAP. While the baby may wish that you would go back and do them again, giving in is going to ruin all your hard work and can make it hard to keep the baby to sleep. Yes, the baby may fuss for a bit but they will adjust and soon they will sleep through the night.

In general, you should handle all the nighttime awakenings that are unrelated to food in the same way that you handled bedtime. If you are working on the SLIP method, you should let the baby navigate these periods independently. You know that they are able to do this since they showed you how they could fall asleep on their own during bed. It just may take a few days before they can get into a routine of falling asleep on their own.

On the other hand, if you chose a SWAP method, you may need to go back into the room and finish that. For example, some parents will rub their baby's back to help them fall asleep with the SWAP method. If this is what you did, then when the baby wakes up again at night and isn't hungry, you will go back in there and rub their back to get them to sleep.

In addition to that information, you may want to consider some of the following guidelines as well:

- If it has only been a few hours since you put the baby down to bed, you should give them some time to resettle down on their own. The compulsion for the baby to just fall back asleep during this time can be potent and sometimes your intervention is going to reinforce their waking. If you give your child some space, they may fall right back to sleep.

- When your child wakes up, your decision tree will rely on two options. The first one is that you go over to your child after giving them five to ten minutes to try and fall asleep on their own. The second is to just wait it out until the baby goes back to sleep without your assistance.

- If you are convinced that your baby is waking up and that you need to interfere, then you must repeat the process that was used during bedtime. As a general rule, before midnight, you will want to have your child go back to sleep without you. But after you get past midnight, it is fine to offer a bit of assistance.

- You should remember to be really stingy when you try to help your child fall asleep during the night. You are changing things up and this is hard for the baby at first but they can handle it. Remember that each time you run into the room to cuddle or bounce your child, you are rewarding them for waking up. We are not trying to be mean here, just trying to make sure that the baby will fall asleep and stay asleep.

- Commit to being less involved each night. This helps the baby adjust to you not doing all the work. For example, if you spent twenty minutes patting their back on one night to get them to sleep, commit to only patting their back for fifteen minutes the next one.

How to Deal with Wakeups Early in The Morning

The biological compulsion to stay asleep is very strong for babies in the evening at bedtime but it does kind of peter out when you get closer to the morning. Many babies are going to wake up early in the morning such as at four or five in the morning simply because their sleep drive is pretty low during this point.

If the baby does wake up at an incredibly early hour, the first thing you may want to try is to see if SWAP or SLIP will be enough to help them get back to sleep until a better time. This is not always going to work for you though. You may have to try it for a few weeks to see but because the compulsion to stay asleep is so low during the morning, it may not work out the way that you want and the baby may want to wake up.

Many parents have found success by giving their baby a quick snack during these early hours. This can help give everyone a few more hours of sleep. Doing this for an hour or so during the morning to give everyone a break is generally not going to ruin all the work that you did all night when it comes to independent sleep. So, go ahead and give them something to eat and maybe spend a few minutes cuddling with them to get them back. Over time, they will learn how to sleep independently, especially if you have kept up with all of the other sleep training techniques that we have talked about.

One thing to remember here is that the goal of independent sleep is not night weaning. Typically, the number of requests that you get at night from the baby to eat is going to diminish quite a bit as they grow older and independent sleep is established. But in the beginning, your child may demand to eat a few times during the night. After some time, as your baby can take in more food during the day and gets on a better schedule, you may decide that it is time to get rid of one or two feedings during the night, and eventually, you will decide to fully night wean the baby.

No matter how well you do with SLIP or SWAP, there are still going to be times when your baby is going to wake up at night. Often this is because they are hungry and you simply need to feed them and they will go back to sleep. Don't fret too much about this. As the baby gets older and gets on a routine with SLIP or SWAP, they will start sleeping completely through the night.

Heidi Oster

Chapter 9:
How to Handle Naptime Troubles

After you have had some time to sleep train your baby during bedtime, it is time to move on and help your baby prepare to sleep during naptimes. Many parents still struggle with this time even after they have been able to get their baby to sleep during the night. Babies of all ages still need to have some quiet time, as well as a naptime, to help them get enough rest during the day. But some children are going to fight against this. Let's take a look at some of the things you should know in order to get started with sleep training during nap time.

When Should Naptime Training Start?

There are three options that you can choose when it comes to nap training. Some parents choose to do the nap training and night training at the same time. They think that because they are already doing the work for one, they may as well do it for both. It can be a bit painful and a big hassle when you are doing them, but it can help maintain consistency and will eliminate any confusion the baby may have. It takes some work, but it can be done if you are consistent and ready for the challenge.

Another option is to do nap training first. Parents who choose this option prefer to work with the naps first and do a test run to see how it all works. However, this is not always the best option. You will find that while babies may automatically fall into a pattern of good naps once you establish a good bedtime sleep, it doesn't go the other way. This means that you may have to do the work twice to get both bedtime and naptime to work for you.

If you are going to do the nap time and bedtime sleep training separately, then you should start with night training first. This is a longer period of time you need the baby to sleep during, and if you can get the baby to sleep through the night, it means that you can finally get the rest that you need. Then, once the baby can sleep through the night, you can handle naptime with a bit more energy.

How to Do Nap Training

If you have already started with a bedtime sleep training routine, and it has worked well for you, then there is no reason why you can't keep this up now that you are moving on to nap time. It is best to stick with the same sleeping techniques if possible because this can avoid a lot of confusion when it comes to your baby falling asleep at night and when it is time to take a nap.

The first thing you need to keep in mind when working on nap time, outside of using the same technique as bedtime, is to follow the natural schedule of your baby. While there are times when this may get messed up such as for vacations or if you had a rocky night of sleep, you want to try to follow the natural rhythms of your baby. Some babies want to take three smaller naps during the day while others will take two bigger naps. Trying to force the baby to take more naps than they naturally want to do can lead to a lot of hard work for you. Follow some of the cues that your baby gives you and work from there to come up with a sleep schedule that works for both of you.

Another thing to remember is that you should never have the last nap be too close to bedtime. It isn't going to work well if your baby is waking up from their nap at six at night, and then you want to get them to bed at seven. The baby, no matter what age, is going to need a good chunk of time between their last nap and when you want them to fall asleep, or they will simply have too much energy to fall asleep. If you want them to bed by seven, the last nap should probably end no later than four, and maybe earlier if the child is a little bit older.

Before laying the baby down for a nap, do some of the same things that you would do for the baby at bedtime. Make sure that you have played with them and gotten them worn out a bit. This can include playing with toys, free play, and spending time outside. Make sure that they have had time to eat as well so they won't wake up hungry later. You can also change them, make sure their clothes and bed are comfy, and that they have everything they need for a safe and comfortable nap time.

When you lay the baby down, it is best to use the same techniques that you use for bedtime training. This includes bringing in some of the sleep tools that we discussed earlier in this guidebook. These sleep tools can sometimes be enough to lull the baby to a good nap time without any added work, provided that you did a good job with sleep training at night. You may need to put in a little bit extra work to get them to fall asleep during nap time than you do with bedtime, but it won't take long to get them ready.

Nap time doesn't have to be a big hassle with your baby. If you have implemented a good sleep schedule with them and you have worked to get your chosen sleep training technique to work for your baby at night time, then nap time won't take a lot of added effort on your part.

Heidi Oster

Chapter 10:
Common Setbacks

While you may have the best intentions when you get started with sleep training, there are times when your baby is not going to go along with the plan that you have set out. They may have anxiety about being separated from you, may run into trouble when you are on vacation, and so much more. Let's look at some of the common setbacks that you may experience during this time and what you can do to prevent it from ruining all your efforts.

Sleep Regression

Every once in a while, no matter how good you are at setting up a sleep schedule with your baby, their sleep will all of a sudden become a big mess. At this time, the baby is going to become fussy as well, which can either be the cause or the result of this sleep deprivation.

Sleep regression can be hard on a parent, but it is perfectly normal in most cases. If the sleep regression is happening because the baby is going through new milestones, going through a growth spurt, or suffering from something like teething, then take heart. They will be over it soon and things will get back to normal.

But, if the sleep regression occurs because you have gotten lax on your sleep training methods and you are just letting the baby sleep however they want, then this can be a problem. You have to maintain the work that you did during sleep training to get the full benefits and to ensure random sleep regressions don't occur to you.

Separation Anxiety
Baby separation anxiety is when the baby fears that when you leave, they are never going to see you again. This can be either when you leave them with another person, or when you go out of the room. Sometimes, it is when the baby wakes up and night and notices that you are no longer there. Observing this behavior can be heartbreaking but take note that it is an important developmental stage for your baby. Through this process, they will learn how to be an independent person.

Separation anxiety is often going show up when the baby is about four to six months and then will peak when the baby is about twelve to eighteen months old. There are some babies who will still suffer from separation anxiety when they are two.

When the baby is first born, they don't know any better. They think that they will never be separated from you. However, at this age, they won't really remember that you exist when it is time to leave the room because they just don't understand how object permanence works. But when the baby reaches four to six months, they are going to learn that you and they are different beings. They will also remember you, even if they are not able to see you. However, at this age, the baby doesn't have the sense of time, nor do they have the experience to know that you will come back soon. To them, they think you will be gone forever.

Feeling anxious is pretty normal for them because they don't feel your security-inducing presence around any longer. You can probably guess that babies who have a lot of separation anxiety near bedtime are ones who will be really hard to settle down for the night. And they will have a ton of trouble self-soothing when they wake up at night.

So, how can you avoid these issues with separation anxiety and your baby? A few things that you can try out will include:

Play Some Games Like Hide and Seek and Peek-A-Boo.
When the baby is only a few months old, start playing these games. You can slowly hide for a bit longer each time. When the baby learns that you will reappear each time this happens, they will quickly learn that you will be back, even during times when they don't see you.

Talk About What You Plan to Do.
You will be surprised at how much babies are able to understand. This is why it is a good idea to let them know what you plan to do when you leave. This helps them to feel less scared.

Don't Dramatize.
It may be hard to leave your baby, especially when they are dealing with separation anxiety but you must act like it is not a big deal. The baby will take their cues from you. If you act like your leaving isn't that big of a deal, then the baby will start to learn that as well.

Share Your Tasks with Another Caretaker.
If it is possible, have someone else help take the baby to bed. This can help the baby get used to the idea that you won't always be doing that for them.

Of course, this is harder when you are breastfeeding since you are the only one who can do this.

Keep Your Promises.
If you place the baby down and they seem nervous, let them know you will be back if they need you. Then come back. Keeping these promises can help the baby feel secure that you won't leave them.

Traveling
If you travel with a baby, just be prepared for some messed up sleeping patterns. This is true while you are gone and probably for a few days after you return. You are taking the baby away from what is familiar to them and they may be anxious and even distracted by all of the new things. It is hard for a lot of adults to stay on a sleep schedule when they travel, so imagine what it must feel like to a little baby who is just getting used to their sleep schedule.

There are a few things that you can do to make sure that your baby is able to sleep well even when you are traveling. Some of the things that you can try out include:

Bring Something That They See as Familiar from Home.
This can make it easier for the baby to fall asleep. It can be the white noise sound they are used to, a stuffed animal, or a favorite blanket, anything that is going to help your baby fall asleep.

Don't Be Too Worried About the Baby Sleeping Outside.

If you are on a vacation, the last thing that you should worry about is having to head somewhere for naptime. Bring along something that is breathable and can go over the stroller and let the baby sleep there. If your baby is able to fall asleep in the stroller at their regular naptime, this is just fine.

Bring A Travel Cot or Someplace Else for The Baby to Sleep.
Even if you are not at home, it is best for the baby to sleep in their own space. Bring along something for the baby to sleep in, or call ahead to your hotel to see if they can provide you with something. Then, when it is time for bed, just follow your regular bedtime and lay the baby down using the same techniques that you used at home.

Don't Get Started with Any New Bad Sleep Habits at This Time.
Just because you are not at home doesn't mean that you should start up some new sleeping habits with the baby. For example, if you don't share a bed with the baby at home, then there really isn't a reason to start this habit when you are on vacation. If you don't rock the baby to sleep at home, then don't do it on vacation. Sure, you will probably have to spend a little longer getting the baby to sleep because of the new location, but stick with what you usually do so that your baby doesn't develop new habits that you have to break later on.

Change in The Time (Daylight Saving Time)
When the time changes during Daylight Saving Time, it can be a nightmare for families, no matter what age their child is. They worry that the time change is going to mess with the sleep training that they have worked so hard on. The baby is not used to this time change but since everything now operates

on this new time change, it is important to get the baby moved over. And it happens two times a year!

The best thing to do with this is to gently move bedtime just a little bit at a time. When the time moves forward or backward, slowly move the bedtime fifteen minutes at a time, in either direction that you need. This isn't such a big change that it is going to ruin all your work but gets the baby on the new time schedule within a week or so.

Unfortunately, there's nothing that you can do to stop the time change, and it is something that every parent has to go through. But with a little planning, and realizing that you may have a few rough nights, you will be able to get the baby on the new schedule.

Your Child Doesn't Nap
Most babies are going to take a nap during the day. They may not take them at the times that you want and sometimes they may not last as long as you would like but most babies can't go more than a few hours without needing to take a nap of some kind. This is a good thing for a parent who needs a break; however, as your child reaches toddler age, they may go through times when they refuse to take a nap. It doesn't matter if mom and dad are exhausted and need a break, and it doesn't matter if the toddler is tired and needs to fall asleep, sometimes they are going to refuse to nap.

If this only happens a few days here and there, it isn't a big deal. But when your child is throwing a tantrum on the floor because they are so exhausted for skipping their naps, you will naturally look for a solution to this issue. The art here comes in the form of using gentle coercion and using it to make a solid and predictable naptime.

While this may sound simple in theory, it can be a struggle. Many families struggle with this and often it is not that big of a deal, other than the parents need a break if the toddler gets enough sleep during the night. To help you determine whether naps are completely gone from your life forever, or if you are just hitting a bump in the road, the two questions that you need to ask right now are how many hours is the child sleeping at night, and are these hours enough.

When we talk about children who are between the ages of two and four, they will need somewhere between 11 to 15 hours of sleep during the day. This is a big spectrum and it will vary based on the child at hand. If your child is on the latter end of this range, your child is probably not going to fight with taking a nap. However, some toddlers will only need the eleven hours at night and it is very rare that they will take a nap.

Now, if we are talking about a baby, you may have to still try to convince them to take a nap. You can utilize some of the sleep training techniques that we have been talking about in the rest of this guidebook to help you gently lull the baby to sleep. And just like how it happened when you did sleep training in the evening and at bedtime, you may have to spend a few days to make this happen.

Even with an older child, you still need to give them some downtime even if they aren't napping. This can be good to calm the child down and can ensure that you also get a break. You can have the child to sit in their room with a few books or some coloring pages and tell them that they must sit in their rooms and be quiet for a bit. Some kids will start to doze off anyway but when the child gets some say in the process, but you still get a little break.

Starting the Day Too Early

Keep in mind that all babies are going to wake up too early, way earlier than the parents would pick if they had a choice. The only question is whether the time is too early for the parent or if it is actually too early for the baby. Babies are going to usually wake up early, often sometime between six and six-thirty in the morning. Some make it even earlier.

Your goal needs to be maximizing the total amount of uninterrupted sleep that your child gets during the night. For most babies, this will be about eleven hours of sleep at night. But there are some babies who are neither getting ten or eleven hours of sleep and they also aren't making it to six in the morning. If your baby is legitimately getting up too early, there are a few things that you can try to get them to stay asleep including:

Make Bedtime Earlier.

Some babies are going to bed too late and this can make them cranky. When they are fussy, they may have a hard time falling asleep and staying asleep in the morning. It may seem counterintuitive but sometimes putting the baby to bed a little bit earlier will get them to sleep later in the day. You can test this out. Try putting them into bed a little earlier for about three to five days and see if it works.

If your baby gets their ten to eleven hours of sleep by four in the morning, it is going to be pretty hard to convince them to go back to bed. You may need to make the bedtime a little later and that could solve the whole problem.

You may need to spend some time experimenting here to see what works the best for the baby and for the parents. You can start out with a later bedtime and see if that solves the problem. If you feel that the baby is getting enough sleep by the time they wake up, then this may be the choice to go with. However, if they aren't getting the ten to eleven hours and are still getting up early, consider moving the bedtime a little earlier and see if that works for you.

Heidi Oster

Conclusion

Thanks for making it through to the end of *Baby Sleep Training*. Let's hope it was informative and able to provide you with all of the tools you need to achieve your goals whatever they may be.

The next step is to utilize some of these methods for your own. Many parents run into trouble when it comes to helping their babies get to sleep. They want to make sure that their baby is getting plenty of shut-eye at night but they also want to be able to do something other than holding the baby the whole night. The techniques that we discussed in this guidebook will help you to finally get your baby to be an independent sleeper.

There are many different techniques that you can choose when it comes to sleep training. You may have to try a few different techniques in order to get your baby to sleep. But with some patience, and by following these techniques, you will be able to get that baby to sleep!

If you find this book helpful in anyway a review to support my endeavors is much appreciated.

Heidi Oster

Baby Sleep Guide to Promote Healthy Sleep Habits

www.ingramcontent.com/pod-product-compliance
Lightning Source LLC
Chambersburg PA
CBHW071159070526
44584CB00019B/2850